BORN ON THE WRONG SIDE OF THE FENCE

Published by
Chi Chi Press

Chi Chi, aka Maurice Elson

"A good little publishing company"*
1-877-711TANK (711-8265)

Copyright © 2023, Chi Chi Press
All rights reserved. To excerpt or reprint any portion of this book please contact Aaron Elson at aaronelson.com or 877-711-8265
ISBN: 978-0-9969602-3-6

* *"Chi chi"* was my mother's term of endearment for my father. One day, when they got a used Mercedes sedan from a relative, my dad called it *"a good little car."* My parents ran a small school transportation company. The illustration was by one of their drivers. – **Aaron Elson, publisher**

BORN ON THE WRONG SIDE OF THE FENCE

Contents

Foreword 3
Dedication 4
Introduction 6
Chapter 1 7
Chapter 2 12
Chapter 3 17
Chapter 4 22
Chapter 5 26
Chapter 6 30
Chapter 7 37
Chapter 8 40
Chapter 9 43
Chapter 10 46
Chapter 11 49
Chapter 12 51
Chapter 13 57
Chapter 14 64
Chapter 15 73
Postscript 78
Post Postscript 80

BORN ON THE WRONG SIDE OF THE FENCE

Foreword

    The story you are about to read would be almost impossible to believe were it not for the almost daily contact through e-mail and telephone over a two-year-span since the fall of 2002. It may be difficult to read for some because of its stark and graphic portrayal of events as they occurred. Mr. Ehlich is gifted with an almost vivid photographic memory and we are the richer for his part in the preservation of history as it occurred in his area of the world in the closing days of the demise of the Third Reich.

    Mr. Ehlich originally made contact with Mr. Dee Eberhart, publisher of the 42nd "Rainbow" Division Regimental Colors, a biannual compilation of stories and letters of interest by veterans of the 242nd Infantry Regiment. His original thought was that men of this division were the liberators of his adopted village in April 1945. Mr. Eberhart's further investigation led to the belief that it may have been the 90th Infantry Division. Since my brother Vern was a replacement in that division I immediately contacted him. The rest is history.

    I am grateful for the friendship of both Bruno and Josie Ehlich. We have been privileged to visit by phone for hours at a time, shared videos of our lives and the almost daily surface and e-mail contact to include photos. I know his story to be true and factual as far as the memory of a 9-year-old would allow under the chaotic conditions endured in the final days of World War II. Vern also saw the result of the tortured victims of the Flossenburg concentration camp. My division history book is replete with firsthand graphic photos of the tragic reality its men experienced as they liberated the Dachau concentration camp in the days following.

    The author welcomes any information historians or veterans may have which more clearly verifies his memory of events and sheds further light on the exact unit that made combat contact in his village.

Glenn E. Schmidt
"A" Company, 242nd Infantry Regiment
42nd Infantry Division

BORN ON THE WRONG SIDE OF THE FENCE

Dedication

This story is especially written to search and to find the whereabouts if possible of the tankers and supporting infantry passing through and occupying Leuchtenburg via Weiden in Bavaria, Germany, approximately in April, May and June of 1945.

This story is dedicated to several friends of mine; firstly to Mr. David Jolliffe of Sydney who encouraged me for years to start writing. Then to God's gift to me. He put me in touch with two gentlemen and veterans of the Second World War. They were right there in the middle of the fighting and also as an extra bonus, right there where I was at the right time and place. They are Glenn and Vern Schmidt of California, USA. Glenn was captured and put into Stalax IXB as a POW. I like to mention here that he was put out of action by a bullet through his helmet. I am thankful he is still here today with us. Then his brother Vern; amazingly his unit was involved with the liberation and rescue of his brother at that same Stalag. Among other things he was involved with the liberation and rescue of the prisoners at the dreaded Concentration Lager Flossenburg; the same Concentration Lager I was forced to visit and to see the end results of that slaughter. It is very hard for me to judge which of the two gentlemen I have to mention here first as both of them did their utmost to make this story fit together. They spent hours of research for me and were it not for them, the first two chapters of this book would never have been written so accurately.

Also, I have to mention here a veteran and his beloved wife who put me in touch with Glenn and Vern Schmidt. Their names are Mr. and Mrs. Eberhart. Many thanks to them. Also involved were Jim and Rhoda Reid of the 90th Division Association. Their help was also very much appreciated.

So what more could I have asked for? All this enormous research and help I received from them 60 years later. Vern was at that time only ten kilometers from Leuchtenburg at a place called Vohenstraus and had seen the same bomber coming down. It had exploded near us the same day. Thankfully all of that crew bailed out and were rescued by Vern's troops. Some of those floating parts of that bomber hit the ground only meters from where I stood. So it is unbelievable that God had put us together 60 years later. Therefore I

BORN ON THE WRONG SIDE OF THE FENCE

am sure that one day I will find out if the tankers and the supporting GIs who poured through our village were with the 90th Division. I think but am not exactly sure that they were supported by M4s of the 761st all-Negro Tank Battalion. Regardless, it is and was the heroic fighting spirit, dedication and unselfishness, disregard of their precious lives that saved me and my family and all those Germans from the evil the likes of Adolf Hitler and those pathetic killers he had with him.

And I would like to mention here that most regular Army Wehrmacht soldiers did recant that war; they were drafted up by the millions and used as cannon fodder and died for Mr. Hitler's dream.

To all those fighting men of the mighty U.S. I bow, as I surely would not be here today if it were not for them and all those Allied forces who assisted them.

I thank Glenn's and Vern's lovely wives for putting up with my interruption and ever-coming questions. I also thank my wife Josie for putting up with me for years. Telling her the same story over and over again. It's a wonder she never put me away. For this I love her.

Then of course I thank Mrs. Evelyn Koop, my typist and editor of this my story. She must be blessed with patience and love as it must have been very hard to create a readable story out of my unprofessional mumbo jumbo. God bless her for all the work she's done. I hope that one day I can meet her and thank her for what she did.

So please read my story which is written for all of you, as I have read hundreds of your fighting stories. I am amazed we are still here to remember. Also still to remember all those who never returned. For those I pray!

In the name of God Jehovah, God bless you all.

Bruno Ehlich, Sergeant (retired) Royal Australian Air Force

BORN ON THE WRONG SIDE OF THE FENCE

Introduction

    Unquestionably, one thing in this world is that one cannot choose his or her nationality, race or time. Therefore I did just that, arriving at 1700 hours on the 20th of March, 1936, into this crazy world, at a crazy time, on the wrong side of the fence!

    I was one of millions. Vienna, Austria, in March of 1936, was in turmoil. The cause was Hitler and his Nazis. Most people today know about this totally absurd time in history which destroyed millions of human beings, shifted thousands onto other continents, split families apart and created the biggest shift of people from one continent to another. Little did I know but I was to be sucked into this mess years later.

Bruno in 1944

BORN ON THE WRONG SIDE OF THE FENCE

Chapter 1

Austria, Germany, Austria

My father, Bruno Ehlich, a mechanical engineer, was at that time 27 years of age. For reasons unknown to me and I never questioned why, my parents lived with my Aunt Rosa, my father's sister, in a beautiful, dainty village called Purkersdorf in the western Vienna Woods. Her home was a very charming villa and we all shared it with her and her husband, Hans Fadaneli, the station master of Unter Purkersdorf (Lower Purkersdorf), 24 kilometers west of Vienna.

Upon my arrival from the Allgemeinde Spital (General Hospital) in Vienna, we moved into the upper floor of this Roman looking sandstone villa.

From the beginning, I was spoiled by my aunt and my nanny, a 20-year-old lady called Hilda. She wheeled me around this huge garden in my pram amongst flower beds, pine trees and oaks. Funny, I never remembered my Mum but I remembered Hilda.

Austria at that time was a country with massive unemployment and political upheaval. Hitler wanted engineers and tradesmen to migrate to Germany to take up jobs mostly in the heavy armaments industries and in early 1937 my father took that chance. My father and mother never owned a home and the shift to Germany was welcomed. Dad was provided with a new apartment in the city of Magdeburg, at 19/1 Felgeieberstrasse, about 60 kilometers west of Berlin on the River Elbe.

On June 14, 1938, my brother Fritz was born. The only negative situation was that our apartment was near a large military airfield which nearly cost us our lives in the later years. This airfield was totally destroyed in the Allied bombing raids. Our apartment received a hit and was partly burned out, but luckily at that time we lived in another part of Germany.

My father started his new job on the 15th of March, 1937, as a mechanical engineer in a factory called "R-Wolf-Bruckau." Dad was really happy with his new job as a design engineer and settled in very quickly. Mum loved her first new home and spent most of her time looking for new furniture. I, with my

BORN ON THE WRONG SIDE OF THE FENCE

one and a half years of age, understandably did not realize what went on in Germany at that time in 1937.

Hitler was now in full control and he and his followers geared the country slowly into a massive war machine. It did not take very long to turn the humble machine manufacturing factory into a tank engine manufacturing plant. Dad now had a complete turnaround from designing sewing machines, etc., to designing tank engines.

Dark clouds were rolling in very fast over Germany. Dad told me after the war that any complaints in public, of any kind, would have landed him for sure into a concentration camp commonly known in Germany as a "KZ." Then on 15 May, 1939, my father was drafted up for military training. He had to report to the Recruiting Center in Blankenburg in the Harz Mountain region in Gottingen for four months up to the 15th of September 1939.

After basic military training, Dad was trained as a tank driver. He later told me that his involvement with the designing of tank engines and his qualifications as a mechanical engineer made him a candidate for what he called Panzer fodder.

Mum was so lonely during his basic military training that she decided to move back to Austria to live with Aunty Rosa for the duration of his training.

On 15 September, 1939, Dad called us and urged us to return very quickly to Magdeburg. His military basic training had ended and he must have known then that at any moment, the greatest war in history was about to unfold. Mum and we children spent a few happy days with Dad. One day in late September, Dad was gone, like millions of other Germans – "To War."

Kindergarten started at four years of age. One day in early 1940, our kindergarten teacher gave us a letter for our mothers. It informed them that all boys and girls had to be dressed in a standard uniform as laid down by the German Hitler Youth Organization. This was as follows: black high laced shoes, white socks up to our knees, black shorts, a four-button coat, white shirt with long sleeves, black tie with a woven Hitler Youth knot made out of split bamboo, and an Adolf Hitler style haircut for boys. We also had a document to state that we came from Aryan stock. It was at this time that I noticed the disappearance of some of my schoolmates. Little did I know of the forced removal of most children with Jewish ancestors or Jewish families to various concentration camps – Buchenwald, Auschwitz, Flossenburg, Treblinka, etc., never to return. We attended with those uniforms and every morning lined up in front of our flagpole with the swastika flag flying and singing our Hitler songs.

BORN ON THE WRONG SIDE OF THE FENCE

One day my mother decided to purchase a tricycle for me and took me to a toyshop. As we entered the shop, my mother, being Austrian, said "Gruss Gott," meaning "Greetings from God," only to be yelled at by some fanatical German saleslady, "Here in this shop you will raise your hand in a German salute and say 'Heil Hitler.' Jawohl! Or I call the Gestapo." Well, my mother responded exactly like she had been instructed and for many days after that incident looked over her shoulder many times. We were issued with gas masks and as my brother had severe asthma and was only a bit over one year old, he went blue in the face and nearly died as Mum attached the mask on his little face. She never tried again after that.

In 1940, one year after my father went to war, he came home on leave for three days. He had survived the Polish and the French campaigns. My brother and I did not recognize him anymore. On the day he had to leave he told my mother that he would not go back to camp and whilst talking to Mum, who had tears running down her face, there was a knock on the door. Dad opened it only to be confronted by two burly leather-coated Gestapo agents. They advised him to be down at the collecting truck in five minutes or be shot as a traitor. Dad put his arms around Mum, gave her a long hug and said to her, "I would rather be shot by some Russians on the front than by Nazis."

A few weeks later Mum screamed the house down and I was told that my uncle – Mum's brother – had been killed on the Polish front; shot in the heart. Later we received news from one of my uncle's comrades advising that my uncle had been shot in the stomach and died in agony. From that moment, Mum lost weight and fretted every day.

The bombing of our city, Magdeburg, started in 1941. I was 5 years old and started to notice the tragic moments in our lives. We children had our kindergarten shifted underground in an old coal cellar. We received our daily quarter-liter of milk from the Red Cross but still lost weight as food was rationed out to families, in smaller and smaller parcels, as the war intensified. Now the English Air Force started to throw toys from their aircraft, like small dolls, writing pens, pencils, etc., with an explosive charge in them. Children picked them up and whilst playing with them, had their fingers or hands ripped apart by the explosions. Those toys were not intended to kill but just to maim the child and put a strain on the German medical system. Medicine, which should have been sent to the soldiers on the front, was now used en masse in the homeland. So we were told never ever to pick anything up, anywhere, just report it to the next police station. Many of my school mates landed in hospital by getting injured by those toys. This was only the beginning of the slaughter;

the slaughter no little boy or girl will ever forget in their life, as death was to come for many, in many different ways.

The thunder started in the morning as we had just enjoyed the meager breakfast, but it was not the thunder of the weather; it was the thunder of many, many British bombers that approached our city. Death was coming fast to many of us. The sirens on top of the buildings wailed mournfully as Mum dragged us down three floors, into our bomb shelter many meters under street level with my little brother in one arm, gas masks around her neck and a bag with a little food and water plus medical supplies. I followed her by grabbing onto her skirt, running along the dark tunnel under our home which was lit up by death head symbols painted on the walls in luminous phosphorous paint, until we came to our shelter.

The shelter was a concrete room of four meters by four meters and three meters high, fitted out with bunk beds around the walls and already occupied by many screaming women with their children and infants. The older people just sat there praying and shaking. Finally the heavy steel door was slammed shut. It had a gas seal so if we got hit it would have prevented smoke and gases from entering our shelter.

The only way out was a half meter by half meter window about one and a half meters above floor level, shut by a steel grid and again by a gas and smoke proof door. To get out if we were still alive after a direct hit was highly unlikely. Those bombs penetrated through meters of solid concrete and by exploding would pulverize everything in the cellar and leave a ten- to fifteen-meter crater. I had seen hundreds of them. If by chance the house got hit and just collapsed, the water mains would break, the gas pipes would burst and water would have flooded the cellar in hours and drowned all of us like rats. It happened to many civilians not only in Germany but also in London and hundreds of other cities which were bombed. Dresden in Germany lost as many as 60,000 civilians in one night bombing by the British Air Force. After the war when bombed-out buildings were excavated, deep down cellars were opened with many skeletons inside. People were drowned, gassed or burned to death as they were unable to escape.

The bombing got heavier day by day during 1942. Not only by day with the Americans but also by night with the British. Night after night Mum dragged us into the cellar and it got so bad that I had nightmares nearly every night. In wintertime especially, the bomb shelter was like a refrigerator. In the mornings when I went to kindergarten I stepped over dead people, blown out of their bombed buildings. No one had time to remove those bodies and there

BORN ON THE WRONG SIDE OF THE FENCE

were hundreds of them. The stench from the burned-out buildings and burned flesh will never leave me.

One day we went to the railway station and a woman was running around with a heavy suitcase. She called out "Hans-Gerda" over and over again. She was really mad, until one German Red Cross Sister stopped her and opened the suitcase and to my horror, with my five years of age, I saw in that open suitcase two burned, shrunken, cooked bodies of two babies. Mum pulled me aside very quickly.

The next day I saw hundreds of burned bodies stacked up near our house and Mum told me that this large Red Cross bunker was hit by phosphorous bombs and they all burned to death. I have seen people stuck into bathtubs, dead, as the side of five-story buildings just blew out and exposed five floors. One could see kitchens, bedrooms, toilets exposed and sheets and blankets, etc., hanging out of them. The streets were covered with all sorts of household goods blown hundreds of meters around. Dead cats and dogs were lying stinking in the streets and gardens. Through all of this mess I still had to attend preschool because every morning we were counted by the teachers and every morning children were missing. One could only guess as to why.

One day the circus came to town with their horse-drawn caravans, fifteen to twenty of them. They put all those caravans in a circle and next erected a tent. During the following night we had an air raid which lasted nearly half an hour and our house got a direct hit in the garden; which not only destroyed the vegetable garden but created a five meter by ten meter hole. But the most horrible sight was a seven meter by fifteen meter hole where the circus caravans had stood. We never found anything; people or horses. There must have been about fifty of them, all obliterated, consumed by a huge fireball. A direct hit by a 500-kilogram bunker buster bomb.

I was only five years of age and I had a little brother, so my mother decided to vacate and we got permission from the Gestapo to travel back to Austria and to live again with our Aunt Rosa. This was only possible because my grandfather was a member of the Nazi party. This move saved our lives as two weeks later, our home in Germany had a direct hit by a phosphorous bomb which burned our top floor out. What remained was stolen.

Chapter 2

Austria

I never saw our home again. Mum went back once and all that was left was our foot pedal sewing machine which she recovered in 1942. So again, on our fourth shift back home to Austria we were living with relatives. I was handed over to my Aunt Anna who had no children and whose husband was in the navy submarines. My brother lived with my grandparents on my father's side. My grandparents on my mother's side lived 30 kilometers south of Vienna, in a place called Weigelsdorf. More about this later.

Move number four, back into the lovely Vienna Woods, back with Aunt Rosa, Uncle Hans and Aunt Anna. Aunt Rosa's children, my cousins Walter and Herbert, now had gone into the Luftwaffe. Herbert went as a pilot and Walter as a rear gunner. Both trained in dive bombers called "Stukas."

At this time I had to live with my mother's sister called Aunt Anna and her husband Hans. They had a little grocery shop not very far away from my Aunt Rosa so I had the good luck to have the best of two aunts living next to each other. As I mentioned, Uncle Hans was a submariner and after his sub was sunk in the English Channel he was one of only five to escape the sinking vessel. He never recovered from the rapid ascent from 30 meters down and had a severe mental condition. Because of this he was sent home to manage his grocery store again. He died of throat cancer after the war.

My cousins Walter and Herbert survived the war. Herbert was shot down over England and became a prisoner of war. He returned to Germany in 1946. Walter was captured by the Americans and returned home in 1946 only to die of cancer in 1991. Herbert is still living in Germany.

I started school in 1942 and witnessed firsthand the burning of all books and literature from the most famous Jewish intellectuals. A high percentage of teachers, doctors, engineers, architects, artists, and religious persons of the Jewish faith were removed and sadly exterminated. Only a few survived the war. In the early years of the Hitler era many Jewish families migrated to different parts of our globe, mostly to the United States of America. Albert Einstein was one of them.

BORN ON THE WRONG SIDE OF THE FENCE

Schooling under the Nazis in 1942 was not easy. Rain or shine, hot or cold, we had to stand on the parade ground and sing our well-trained Nazi songs. We, at the age of six, had to greet, every time you passed a teacher, with a loud "Heil Hitler!" or the cane was given. Heil Hitler in the morning; Heil Hitler in the evening. School started at eight in the morning and finished at four in the afternoon with one-hour midday for lunch and listening to German military music. On Saturday we had to attend school until midday and in the afternoon it was straight to the Hitler Youth camp for training.

We all sat at a large table and had to stick live ammunition into metal belts and these were sent straight to the battle front or training camps around Germany. Talk about slave labor, but we loved it, anything for our beloved Fuhrer. Funny, but one thing stuck in my mind: The rifle cartridges had wooden projectiles, not copper and lead bullets as normal infantry ammunition has, and they all had different colors. Some of them were hollowed out and had phosphorous or other chemicals in them. God only knows. Some were solid wood. I also noticed at that time that the cartridges, usually in brass, were actually just plain steel cartridges.

In the later months we changed to 20mm cannon ammunition. Again we stuffed the cartridges with cordite sticks and crimped the projectiles into them. But, as young as we were, we also did some silly things. We took cannon cartridges, filled them up with cordite, put a woolen wick in them and crimped them closed. We then went up to our castle and lit the fuses and threw them into the gardens below, where they exploded with an almighty bang and frightened the people in the village out of their wits. From then on, all cartridges were counted and we boys had a lovely forced march to do, in rain and thunder, and a big hiding from Mum.

Thousands of schoolchildren had to work on Saturdays for the war effort. Reward, well, if you did well you received a lovely shiny badge you had to wear to inspire the other children and Mum. So the months wore on and we learned marching, climbing, crawling and, you would not believe it, shooting with small caliber rifles – at six years of age!

One day we heard this almighty bang and as we left school on our way home I witnessed the most horrible scene of my life. A military train, returning from the Russian front and loaded with hundreds of wounded German soldiers, hit an outgoing German troop transport train head-on. As the two steam engines compacted with each other, one of the boilers exploded on impact and cooked the driver and fireman instantly and one of them was ejected onto the footpath minus his top torso. On the other locomotive the fireman got pushed into the firebox by the forward pushing coal and was consumed instantly. One hundred and fifty soldiers were killed outright and hundreds mortally injured as most of them were entombed in the overturned carriages.

We schoolchildren were ushered quickly past the scene and I heard the screaming and moaning only 20 feet away. What stuck most in my young mind were the soldiers running around with collected body parts and line after line of stacked dead bodies. What really topped the lot was the almighty bang and shock wave as the other boiler blew up and sent all of us children and adults flying. I landed in some neighbors' front garden with a few bad scratches and could not hear until some hours later.

The investigation which followed was conducted by the Gestapo. My uncle, who was the station master in Purkersdorf, found that the rail points had been shifted as this part of the rails were used as a crossover shunting stretch. This was told to me later, after the war, again by my Uncle Hans as I told him my experiences from my younger years. They never found the culprit but Uncle Hans told me that days after the accident 300 Jewish families were deported to a concentration camp and some communists were shot in revenge.

Winter 1942 was a bad one in Europe and my brother Fritz suffered so much with asthma that my mother applied to the relevant German office to be evacuated to a better climatic area. The climate around Vienna was too detrimental for my brother's health. Once again we were on the move, for the fifth time. The saddest thing of all was that we had not seen our father since 1940.

My mother followed my father around when he was on leave from the Army. Hitler, in the last stages of the war, preferred that most soldiers who were due for recreation leave spend their time in an occupied country other than the German Reich. This was because the soldiers would have seen the tremendous damage done to the cities and factories and they would also have been told about the massive death rate amongst the civilian population and would then have spread this bad news amongst the soldiers on the front.

One of those sad stories which came to light after the war was told to me by a Polish prisoner after he was rescued from the concentration camp Lager Treblinka. A woman and her children, a girl aged six and a boy aged four and a half, received a letter from the Russian front in which her husband, a high ranking officer, asked her to meet him in Warsaw, Poland, to spend his recreation time with her and their children. This officer had not seen his wife

BORN ON THE WRONG SIDE OF THE FENCE

and children for two and a half years. He had been severely wounded, losing an arm in combat, and, of course, had not told this to his wife at the time.

Excited about meeting her husband, she packed her suitcase and a large box of goods like bacon, cheese, ham, etc., for him and his mates on the notorious Russian front. Also included were letters from wives and girlfriends which were to be given to comrades in his unit.

On arriving at the railway station with her children, she was confronted with a band playing military music. The train itself was covered with flowers and streamers; the joyful atmosphere had her heart racing. She asked one of the passengers if this was the right train to Warsaw, Poland, and she was told "yes."

The train departed with the strains of "Deutschland, Deutschland uber alles." The hundreds of men, women and children of all ages on board should have raised some warning and suspicion in her but in all this excitement, she never considered that anything was strange on this train. Firstly there was not a soldier to be seen or any Nazi officials. After the departure she asked a young man where all those people were going to and was told they were all Jews and were going to Poland to be resettled. At that point she started worrying and considered getting off that train at the next stop, but the train never stopped; it continued on for six hours. Finally, deep into the night, they pulled into some railway siding and harsh voices commanded them to leave all belongings on the train and to line up outside on the platform, women and children to the left, men on the right. They all started to wonder why all this?

At this point this woman and her children approached a high ranking German officer and told him that she was on the wrong train and she was on her way to see her also high ranking officer husband on leave in Warsaw. The officer inspected her papers and told her, "Sorry, Mitgegangen Mitgefangen," you went with us, now you are not allowed to leave. She must have, at that point, realized that she was actually transported to a concentration camp.

Later, after the war, this Polish ex-prisoner who overheard all this and, of course, by a miracle survived, told the American Red Cross officer that she was separated from her five year old boy and with her daughter landed up in the gas chamber that night with the Jewish resettlers. All that was left in the morning was the ashes. The boy was never found. (For reference, read the story about the concentration camp Treblinka). By some miracle, her luggage with her name was later found. Would she have been released and reunited with her husband and then told him what she had seen in that concentration

BORN ON THE WRONG SIDE OF THE FENCE

camp? Had this been spread around it would have had all sorts of consequences for the Nazi Party.

This was told to me just after the war and I always connect this story with my mother chasing my father around. Well, that's love I suppose! Mum saw my father, but we children nearly forgot how he looked. Photographs and letters hardly made up for the real thing. We were lucky that he finally came home at all and that he survived this carnage.

Vienna at the end of World War II. *Histclo.com*

Chapter 3

Bavaria, Germany, 1943

We said goodbye to my Aunt Rose and Aunt Anna, taking our very few belongings, only three suitcases full of personal clothing, etc. We left Vienna in May 1943. I was seven years old and my brother Fritz four and a half. At the age of seven I had seen so many bad things I was longing for something nice. I longed for my father and I longed to be together with Mum for longer periods, and I expected this with our move to Bavaria.

All railway stations were full of German soldiers either going to or returning from the battlefields. Not many civilians traveled around in those days. Trains were strafed by Allied fighter planes or blown up by saboteurs, so actually getting to your destination was pure luck. Trains sometimes got rerouted or stopped for long periods of time to load or unload soldiers, or the Gestapo or SS were looking for spies or escaped prisoners of war or Jews.

It took us nearly 22 hours to arrive in Weiden in Bavaria, called by the locals "die Oberpfalz." Mum had some food with her that Aunt Anna gave us from her shop, like ham, bacon, marmalade and ersatz Kaffee (coffee made from barley grain).

On arrival in Weiden we took a bus to our final destination, Leuchtenburg, a small village of about 80 farms gathered around a semi ruin of the Castle of Leuchtenburg. From Weiden to Leuchtenburg it took nearly one and a half hours for the 20 kilometers. Leuchtenburg is on top of a mountain, about 300 meters above sea level. The bus, overloaded with farmers, soldiers and equipment, nearly did not make it to Leuchtenburg as the wood-fired boiler stopped many times and had to be refueled with small logs. Sometimes we all had to get out and push the bus over the next hill.

Finally, after nearly 25 hours of traveling, we arrived in Leuchtenburg, our new home for the next two and a half years. The village of Leuchtenburg dates back to about 900 AD and is clustered around the castle. In 1943 the village population amounted to about 1,000. Ninety percent of its residents were farmers and tradespeople, like blacksmiths, bakers, butchers, storekeepers, council employees and of course the village priest and his staff.

BORN ON THE WRONG SIDE OF THE FENCE

I had never seen a cow pulling farm wagons loaded with hay, etc., which had been harvested from the fields around this lovely cobblestone village. My brain was rattling in overdrive, so much to see, so much to investigate. For a seven year old city boy it smelled like adventure; there was the misty Black Forest which surrounded this magical little village with its babbling brooks and moss covered rocks and especially this eerie old castle with its dark dungeons and tales about ghosts and spells. Wow, what a time I imagined we would have! But reality came down like a brick, hitting me on the head. The bus stopped at the only country pub in that village called "Gasthof zum Burgrug" (Hotel Castle Mug). This hotel was attached at that time to the castle itself and also by an underground passage which had caved in long ago, or had it? The hotel was, and still is today, three stories high. At that time in 1943 it had a large three-story high barn attached with a beer garden in the front in which stood a massive chestnut tree about 400 years old. The barn, beer garden and tree were removed in the 1960s and replaced with a garage, storeroom and discotheque.

In the beer garden there were benches and tables, and locals, tourists and soldiers sat under the shade of this magical old tree, drinking and eating. The owners of the hotel were Mr. and Mrs. Kraus, an elderly couple with two sons and one daughter. The sons were killed in the last stages of the war in 1945 along with their father.

We were received with smiles and love and, being the only refugees in the village at that time, we were quite a novelty. Mr. Kraus allocated us a room on the first floor above the beer hall. The room was two and a half meters wide and five meters long with a window overlooking the main street. One door directly opposite the window opened to a passage that led downstairs into the beer garden. The room had a wardrobe, two single beds, a cot, a little woodstove, a table, and three wooden chairs. That was all for two years. No running water, no tap, no sink, no refrigerator, no cupboards; nothing. Mum and I had to carry the water up in a bucket and we boys had to learn very quickly that we had to go to the woods to collect firewood for the stove and bring it upstairs. Prior to that we had to chop it up so it fit into the little stove.

The first few nights Mum pushed those single beds together so we kept each other warm until she could arrange bedding for us all. Only God knows how she did it. I only remember Mum cried a lot in those nights. I cannot ever remember her cuddling me and I still have no recollection of ever being cuddled or kissed, though she looked after us two boys like diamonds. Thinking back today, it must have been hard for her, coming from a rich

BORN ON THE WRONG SIDE OF THE FENCE

family to this standard, only because of one fanatical "Herr Hitler" trying to create Lebensraum (invading other countries to expand the Reich).

Next we had to report to the headmaster of the village school. I was totally confused by the dialect these Bavarian people spoke as it was like getting myself transferred into the jungle of Senegal. I could not understand 80 percent of what he told my mother. I spoke the Viennese Austrian dialect which, thank God, is nearly 15 percent Bavarian and then I spoke perfect Berlinerish having lived only 60 miles south of the German Nazi capital. Not bad for a child of seven.

Mum was given a sort of slate board, yes, slate like slate on roofs, just with a wooden frame about 25 centimeters by 28 centimeters, a box of chalk, a grammar book and one mathematics book and, of course, a Nazi song book. Lastly a copy of the Hitler Youth code of conduct was also given. The instructions were that I had to arrive by eight in the morning exactly and stand, rain or shine, with all the other children in front of this huge flagpole to receive our daily speech about our glorious Herr Hitler and our glorious army (which was by this time decimated in Russia by the thousands and retreating). Then we had to sing this Horst Wessel song. Of course I had no idea about the words as this had never happened to me before. Our hands were raised in a Hitler salute and then we marched into our classroom which was covered with all sorts of Nazi items and the photograph of Adolf Hitler hanging above the blackboard.

Every classroom was heated in the winter. Sometimes with those dreadful snowstorms raging, we arrived wet and soggy and we had to take our shoes off and put them in front of this huge stove which was fed by the students with pine logs that we had to bring to school ourselves. Seating for the students – 20 of us girls and boys – were small wooden benches attached to tables with a slanted top which one could lift up to store the books; but the worst situation was that it sat two students per bench and table, disregarding the body size of each.

My fellow student was of course a huge 9-year-old well-fed farmer's boy. He looked me up and down and said, "Well, you Ostmark Schwein," which translated meant "Well, you Eastern pig," Austria of course being east of Germany. So I learned in my seven years what it meant to be a refugee in a foreign country. Hitler had Austria annexed into the German Reich but this had little understanding with these Bavarians. I was small and skinny but still I said that he himself looked like an overfed pig. Well, this boy did the worst thing anyone could do to such a small boy as myself. He dobbed me in to the

BORN ON THE WRONG SIDE OF THE FENCE

teacher and in front of 10 girls and 10 boys I received the cane across my bottom 10 times and then I had to stand for a full hour in the corner of the classroom with my nose touching the wall. That was my first day in a Bavarian Nazi-run school!

Lunch was a slice of bread with an apple Mum pinched from a farmer's tree and still today, 50 years later, that is my favorite meal! Poor Mum, only God knows how she did it. At 4 o'clock school was finished and we had to salute the flagpole and yell Heil Hitler. I then walked one kilometer home to our small room, and started homework for school and homework for Mum – like running to the woods collecting firewood and picking mushrooms for the evening meal, including stinging nettles we used to make the spinach and berries. We walked miles on Sundays to collect this type of food and collect firewood for the winter. Mum dried the mushrooms and boiled the berries and other fruits for jam. As we settled in, Mum made some dolls out of rags and stuffed them with sawdust, then painted them with colored pencils. She then walked for kilometers around the farms and the village to trade them for food.

Life was hard for me at that time in 1943 as my life was "school, discipline, work and more work at home." I had to be the man in the family as my brother was ill with asthma and could not at that time be without medicine and could hardly walk or run. At times when we had nothing to do, I took him into the woods and laid him on some nice moss near my favorite stream and collected some berries for him. I told him stories about our father we never knew and that one day we would be back in Vienna. He smiled at me and hugged me often, he with the blond hair and pale face. I carried him on my back until my spindly little legs could not stand it any longer, then I would sit him down and we would lie in the cool green grass in the forest, listening to the cuckoo birds. Mum never worried about us as she knew that even at my little age, I had a grown man's heart and a survival instinct, which I have never lost.

What really stood out in that village was that nearly every house had a swastika flag flying, especially the Gestapo and Army headquarters opposite our hotel. The roof of that building was about level with our living quarters in the hotel and only 25 feet across the street. Bavaria had always been the beehive of the Nazi movement but in Leuchtenburg, it really topped the lot. The castle Leuchtenburg, remote from everywhere, on top of this mountain and surrounded by this tiny village, was quietly used by the SS for the storage of all confiscated goods and belongings taken away from the Jewish families as

BORN ON THE WRONG SIDE OF THE FENCE

they arrived at the concentration camp Flossenburg, for shooting and cremation.

The Flossenburg concentration camp

Chapter 4

1943

Finally war had followed us again but now I was eight years of age and my brother six and a half and we noticed and understood now what this was all about. Even at my age, I absorbed every moment of these turbulent times. Later, in my forties and fifties, I actually realized I had a photographic brain so I just tapped into it and all these memories came flooding back like magic.

In spring 1944 the Gestapo brought French prisoners from the KZ Flossenburg to do work around the village as most able-bodied German men were drafted into the army. The farm work was done mostly by the women of the village so the use of the prisoners was a welcome gift for them. The prisoners were watched by older armed civilian guards, all of them, of course, Party members and all also involved in shady deals with the camp commanders. An uncle of mine told me in later years what actually went on behind the scenes in the Party. Most ordinary Germans suffered badly during the war but Party officials in higher positions were involved in some very bad dealings, especially when it involved the confiscated belongings of the shot and murdered Jews and prisoners of the KZ Flossenburg, 30 miles from here. One day my mother was allocated a French prisoner to help in cutting down one pine tree in the woods. To tell this in a more detailed funny story, we here in this village were given one five-meter pine tree for cutting down and storing for firewood once only and one tree per year.

This tree was picked out by a Party member known as Flur Wachter under the Forest Warden. His nickname was Kurzwatmichel Himmelhergot Scaramenter but his real name was Josef Bausch. One tree per year per family was not enough to cook and heat, especially in winter with up to two meters of snow and icy winds blasting down from the north. We then had to collect every scrap of timber that fell off the trees in the woods, especially the mostly loved pine cones, on weekends. During the summertime they dropped by the thousands in the forest so we kids chased them up, especially after some windy days, and Mum rewarded us with cookies for a few buckets full of pine cones. Also in our spare time we collected berries and mushrooms.

BORN ON THE WRONG SIDE OF THE FENCE

So our French prisoner, his guard, Mum, my brother and I went out to the woods to inspect our tree and cut it down into one meter long sections. It was then marked and piled up for us to collect in due time with our little hand cart made by one of Mum's friends. In those hard times you would think that someone would steal these piled-up wood heaps but this never happened. There were hundreds of those stored woodpiles but they were never touched by anyone. I think the thought of landing in one of the concentration camps stopped a lot of crime from happening during the war times.

Our French prisoner was cutting with Mum, back and forth the saw went, the guard sitting on a rock with his pistol handy in his belt, eating his lunch. Feeding the prisoner was Mum's duty, as she later did. During a whispered conversation whilst sawing, Mum told me after the war, the prisoner asked Mum to bury some civilian clothing near the fallen tree because it was his intention to escape in the following days and he would be so grateful for it and after the war if he got safely away he would thank Mum a thousand times over.

Mum told him yes, she would do it. A few days later my father's suit was gone. God must have been with the prisoner because he made it back to France. We only received one thank you letter years after the war. How this letter found us I will never know, maybe Mum told him her name, God only knows.

The farms in our village and all around in Germany had a lousy time during the war. The Nazi Party officials went to every farm and selected cows, pigs, chickens, etc., putting an official Nazi tag on them. Then at a given time these animals had to be slaughtered and the meat had to be delivered to the Burgomeister's office. These contributions were supposed to be for the armed forces on the front, but the Party officials looked extremely well fed. At the same time most German civilians starved, especially the children.

One day my mother made jam from the berries we had collected in the woods. I said to Mum, "Please let me have some," but she said, "No Bruno, we save it for the winter and don't ask me again." As she went out for a while I quickly spread some on a slice of bread, then turned it around so that the dry side was looking upwards and as Mum passed me in the hallway on the way out, she said to me, "Good boy, Bruno." However, as I entered the outside yard, I took my first bite and received a large bee sting on my tongue. The bee had been resting underneath on the jam. My throat swelled up and I started choking. A German soldier rushed me to the German military hospital just next to us where they inserted an air tube into my throat and stopped my

BORN ON THE WRONG SIDE OF THE FENCE

tongue from slipping back into my throat. It nearly cost me my life for not obeying my mother.

Slowly we settled in and the harsh winter of 1944-45 slowly gave way to spring. But changes had happened in our little village with more and more German troops coming, and one day they occupied our hotel, and even installed their own field kitchen in the cow barn. Some of the soldiers actually gave me some of their field rations which I gave to my Mum to share with her and my brother.

After the army arrived the food supply for us got better day by day as Mum did some ironing for the officers, including mending and washing. My schooling was getting better but not for long as one day one of the Gestapo arrived and asked for 10 boys as volunteers for the army. They needed help in putting rifle and machine gun ammunition into clips and belts and also running between trenches they had dug around the village with water and rations for the soldiers. So war was actually coming to our village. I was detailed with another older boy to run telephone wires up to a command post which was right on top of the castle's main tower. A very fine observation platform from which to watch the advancing Americans.

In 1944 schooling had ended and the school closed down. Most of us eight year old boys now worked for the army. Mind you, it was fun, not hard, but we missed our schooling. Once on a Sunday morning as my brother and I were lying in our favorite place near a mossy long rock in the woods, staring up into the blue sky, we heard a rumble approaching we had never heard before in our lives. Being used to bombing raids and actually having been bombed out ourselves, my thought was that this could be one of those raids approaching our village, so we took off to warn Mum. However, we did not get very far as suddenly, whoosh, a German Messerschmidt bf 109, which was being chased by an American fighter, thundered about 50 feet above our heads. It threw us boys into the "thank God" mushy ground where we lay and watched the aerial battle of bombers and fighters. Death was raining down on us, but we just lay there astonished, watching parachutes opening and planes coming down in flames. A large bomber exploded right above us.

Amazingly, this was later confirmed in 2003 by Vern Schmidt of the 90th Infantry Division. But as metal items like external fuel tanks rained down on us, we made a hasty retreat under some large rocks. It lasted about 20 minutes and then it was all over. Only the smell of burned rubber and oil hung over the woods.

BORN ON THE WRONG SIDE OF THE FENCE

I collected some of those shiny aluminum strips which came floating down on those little parachutes used to confuse German radar. We showed what we had collected to the Gestapo officers, including one damaged fuel tank; one of those long range fuel tanks ejected during aerial fighting by the American and English fighters. We actually got a slap on our back and another of those pathetic little metal badges.

Leuchtenburg Castle. *Credit: Wikimedia Commons*

Chapter 5

Last Days of the War, 1945

In late April the strength of the German military in Leuchtenburg was nearly doubled. Mostly infantry, SS and Gestapo; especially around the Castle, which was heavily guarded. We did notice a lot of trucks entering and leaving which brought in many prisoners from the concentration camp. These prisoners started digging trenches around Leuchtenburg and then we knew that we were preparing for the battle of Leuchtenburg, sooner or later.

One day Mum and my brother were sitting around our kitchen table having our lunch. It was composed of potato soup and bread which we received from an elderly kind German infantry cook. We heard this strange "wobble wobble" noise approaching. Little did we know but death was just about to miss us by 25 meters. The flash accompanied by this tremendous bang and following concussion completely ripped our window out of the wall and the concussion lifted my mother, brother and me out of the chairs and threw us against our kitchen door. The table landed on top of us and the window and hundreds of glass shards and splinters landed on top of the table.

Life stopped for many seconds. I did not realize what had happened until Mum, who was covered in a potato soup and glass mixture, dragged my brother and me out of the rubble. Mum did not say anything; she was pale and shaking. Then we heard the siren going off and we stormed downstairs out into the open. Mum was immediately led away by the Red Cross sisters and my brother was taken to the military hospital next door. However, little me at nine years old, was given a metal bucket to join the bucket brigade to extinguish the fire that raged through the roof of the Gestapo headquarters.

So, why did that shell hit the Gestapo HQ and burn the roof out but do little other damage except to have nearly killed my family and me? First, the U.S. must have had a very good intelligence system; and second, an excellent marksman to hit that building in the middle of the village without doing much damage to anything else. My answer is that they knew that the Castle was stuffed from top to bottom with all the confiscated goods and artifacts from the murdered inmates and locked up victims from those nearby concentration

BORN ON THE WRONG SIDE OF THE FENCE

camps. These goods included fine art, paintings, silver, jewelry, gold, diamonds, porcelain items, fine gold and silver cutlery, etc. Even today Germany is searching for all of those lost and stolen items. Many will never be found as they were mostly buried in caves, mines or sunk in the depths of lakes and rivers. Some of the goods were shipped out and hidden in foreign countries.

The American forces must have obtained this information and therefore did refrain from bombing or shelling the castle. The castle had a very fine observation tower. It had hundreds of German troops stationed there. Why was the village only hit once during the war? The Americans must have known about that booty. Someone must have told them, perhaps an escaped prisoner or a German with a guilty conscience.

During my stint in the Castle, I saw dozens of trucks being unloaded and later, in the last days, being loaded again. God only knows where all this booty was shipped. After the war ended, rumor was that lots of gold jewelry was deep down in the castle. Well, it could have been. Many times we boys looked down into the well only to see the murky waters and lots of military junk floating around – mostly discarded uniforms, caps, etc. God only knows what was underneath this slime.

But back to our burning Gestapo HQ. By the direction from which this artillery or tank shell came, we knew that it was only a matter of days before the Americans would storm Leuchtenburg. School had now been suspended and we boys from the age of eight to 16 years had to help the army. The fun was over. I was detailed to run telegraph wires up into the castle tower where the army installed an artillery command post. I also had to observe the military advances of the U.S. Army, now only kilometers away. It may seem strange but 50 years later, my American friend Vern Schmidt told me that they were seeing us from the town of Vohenstraus, 10 kilometers away. I was right after all. The U.S. Army was only kilometers away.

Later in April, we had to help in running telephone wires into the trenches. My brother was standing in a trench, leaning against a skinny tree. He was only six and a half years old. He took a dive into the trench as a bullet carved a neat one-inch hole two inches above his head and into that skinny tree trunk. Today, 50 years later, I can still hear the sickly ssshippp as the bullet hit. Well, my brother and I took off. We ran the one kilometer up to the village absolutely flat out. My brother nearly passed out with his asthma as we ran up to the army headquarters to report the incident.

BORN ON THE WRONG SIDE OF THE FENCE

By now, the SS had seen the American GIs advancing up the slopes but to my amazement they packed up and started to vacate the village. Now the last remaining SS troops commanded three of us boys and a 20-year-old soldier to man this small anti-tank gun. This was called by the Germans the "Door Knocker" as the small projectiles mostly glanced off the heavy tank armor while scarcely scratching the hull.

We boys and our soldier placed this small artillery piece about 100 meters from the bridge across the River Luhe, then hid amongst the pine trees. My job was to bring the requested shell from the ammunition dump 20 meters from the gun to the loader posted at the gun. The ammunition itself was in wooden cases and every case had different shells in them. There were shells with those glassy looking green tips, red tips and yellow tips. I was told never ever to drop one of them onto that glass tip as the resulting explosion would have killed most of us.

Anyhow, we heard a rumbling noise coming from around the bend and then the first Sherman tank was approaching the bridge. Why in God Almighty did they attempt to cross that bridge without first checking for mines or explosives? No, they were coming right for it.

Our gun commander had this tank in his sights. He was cursing the gun; he was elevating the barrel and then he commanded "Loading!" The shell went into the breach. By then my nine year old heart was pounding as I was watching this, as if in slow motion, from 20 meters away. "FIRE!" yelled the young commander. The shell left the barrel and seconds later hit the Sherman tank. The shell glanced off the tank and exploded into an enormous ball of fire and smoke near the tank. All I remember is our commander yelling for a yellow tip shell and next I was airborne. I never heard the bang. All I remember was hitting a tree and then rolling into a bush meters away from where I had been.

Standing up in agony I noticed our gun upside down and all four crew amongst the wreckage. The Sherman was now about 50 meters away with the turret open and I could see the gunner in the turret. As there was no movement in the bodies, I took off, racing up towards the Castle. I knew that no tank could chase me up this hill as it was covered with meter-high granite rocks and was very, very steep.

On reaching the top and nearing the Castle, especially around the Nazi HQ, I could see they were packing up. The remaining SS and army troops were racing around, loading up their gear and weapons. I was told by one Nazi official to make my way up to the Castle tower and to start rolling up the

BORN ON THE WRONG SIDE OF THE FENCE

wires. All of a sudden the troops started burning their uniforms and destroying official documents in the middle of town. How funny this seemed to me.

Now, hardly any village people were to be seen and under orders I ran up towards the Castle, and through the Castle gate. Up there, I was nearly run over by a large German army truck loaded to the hilt with stolen goods. Not knowing what I should actually do, I raced up into the tower. Not a German soldier was to be seen. Then the bullets and shells started zipping around amongst the castle walls. I hid under some heavy crates. Standing there, I decided to run back into the village. I ran through the castle gate and that was when I was hit in my right arm. My arm dangling and blood spurting, I noticed a metal object sticking out of my lower arm. Running out of the castle I was followed by some GIs who were coming over the walls like monkeys. How I never got killed puzzles me even today but being so small and frail and only nine years old, I must have been spared by the GIs. Then, as I rounded the corner near the church, into the main road, I ran directly into a huge GI from the 90th Division. He lifted me up and I stared into his painted face. He had me by the throat and yelled, "Where are all the village people, BOY?" The war was over for me; I had survived – a nine year old boy with one wounded arm. Lucky! Most of my friends gone, killed for what? For some hilarious little comic called Hitler. However, this is life, "born on the wrong side of the fence."

Chapter 6

Leuchtenburg Liberated, April 1945

This angry and shouting (in English) GI had me now by the shirt and dragged me from the church corner to the middle of the road leading to our hotel. Left and right were GIs kneeling or standing with their weapons trained onto every window or door near us. To my amazement, there stood in the middle of the road this huge Sherman tank; clustered on top were about 10 GIs. I can never forget their white eyeballs staring at me out of their dirty faces. Fifty years later my friend Vern in America told me that they did not wash sometimes for ten days when in battle. Now a GI was approaching me accompanied by a lady U.S. Army officer. She spoke a funny German dialect which I scarcely understood; it sounded like "WHO SIND ALLE LEUTE KLEINER BUB?" (Where are all the village people, little boy?)

The big GI's hand went straight up to my neck and slightly pressed on it. He smiled and passed to me with the other hand a piece of chocolate, which I had not seen for years. Calming down now, I took more notice of what that lady officer had asked me. Then I heard a screeching noise coming out from our hotel. Suddenly Mrs. Kraus, the hotel owner and mother of the dead boy, came storming out from the barn where she had been hiding with a Luger pistol in her hand, yelling, "Where are my boys?" (naturally in German). "Where is my husband?" She was pointing her pistol at the tank. To my amazement a very young GI ran up to her from behind and grabbed the gun from her. What a heroic act! But Mrs. Kraus, mentally deranged, had not seen anything except the huge tank which stood before her.

Again the lady officer insisted with a half-English-German voice: "Who sind alle leute?" but no more "little boy," and no more chocolate. No, now it is a serious matter and the grip of the GI's hand tightened around my neck. Spontaneously my answer was "Under the hotel." His grip loosened and I was told to show her where the 90 percent of Leuchtenburg's inhabitants had fled. My mother once told me that in case something like this happened, we would all go to the old tunnel passage which led from the castle to our hotel. It was partly caved in and had caves leading away from the main passage. These caves were storage areas for potatoes and sugar beets.

Inside the hotel's main entrance was a heavy oak door with rusty hinges and enormous locks. Once down the steps, worn out by nearly 500 years of use, was what seemed to be a four foot wide tunnel passage and 30 feet further

BORN ON THE WRONG SIDE OF THE FENCE

down on the left extended two caves with gothic ceilings. All of the walls in these caves were made of huge stones, carved out from the mountains hundreds of years ago, and were now filled to the brim with the Leuchtenburg elderly and young people. Most able-bodied men were on the front fighting or dead or lucky enough to be a prisoner but not so lucky if in Russian hands.

As my brother and my mother were down there in that cellar, I feared to be severely punished for having given away that hiding place. Sooner or later they would have had to come out of hiding, especially as there were a lot of infants among them.

I felt the GI's grip tighten more and more, virtually lifting me off the ground. Hundreds of eyes were staring at me. I am the only and I mean the only person who was seen in the street. Mrs. Kraus was led away by the Red Cross sister to the vacated German hospital next to our hotel. Leading the whole bunch of GIs and officers through the main hotel entrance, I pointed to that five foot high by three foot wide door. They knocked on it with their rifle butts. The lady officer yelled in her pathetic half German/half American voice, "Aufmachen schnell, Americans hier."

Nothing happened. They looked at me. I looked at them. Then I nearly fainted as the GI dropped me on the ground and then fired with his machine gun into the wooden door. There were splinters everywhere, bullets whistling around us, some coming from the other side of the door passing through to our side. The GI's bullets passed down through the door into the passage.

Nothing happened for a while and then the door sprung open. We heard the women screaming down there with someone yelling, "Okay, we come up."

To my surprise, a very old German man, in his German "Volksturm" uniform appeared. (The last defense used by the Nazis were old men, 60 to 70 years old, and very young boys like myself, as cannon fodder). As he approached, he held his German Schmeisser machine gun over his head and was leading about 200 people out of the cellar, among them my mother and brother. The GIs took this old man's weapon and led him away. (He was released later.)

Each woman coming up had to surrender all items carried in their hands. This of course also affected my Mum because she carried a dish of eggs. These did not belong to her but those eggs were stored below in the cold cellar so she took them anyway. Mum noticed that those GIs took everything away from them and dropped the lot on the ground. I never found out why this happened or why she was so angry about giving them to the GIs. Or, did she really drop those eggs because she was so nervous?

BORN ON THE WRONG SIDE OF THE FENCE

I was pushed to the front and all of those people were marching up and could see me in my Hitler Youth uniform and they all called me "VERRATER" (Dobber). What choice did I have? None. One old woman hit me right in the face. As I found out later, she had lost her only son on the Russian front. Mum stopped her hitting me but was nearly attacked herself by more women calling her an "Ostmarkschwein" (Eastern pig). Again that hate towards Austrians and Hitler being an Austrian and we were the only Austrians in that village. I said Bavarians at that time were fanatic Nazi followers, but not all, I found out later.

Eventually the whole cellar was cleared. Women with infants up to three years were led away, again to the military hospital next door. The remainder had to sit down on the benches in the beer garden surrounded by lots of GIs. The interpreter, now with her pathetic broken German language, had by now settled down. To my surprise, she turned out to be a nice, friendly person or she just acted like it, to calm the people down.

The women and children were separated from the men and then the whole bunch of us were transferred to the church to be locked up for days until everyone answered many questions. This was a very long interrogation. Nobody was allowed home to their residences at all. We were fed, clothed, washed and disinfected with Lysol or DDT, as body lice and fleas were out of control.

Unfortunately, it was April. It was the end of winter and icy cold; therefore a lot of the elderly became ill, and had the U.S. Army not looked after us so well, some of us would have surely died. Even today, I think of those millions of poor, poor Jews and other prisoners and their infants dying in the concentration camps because of the cold and having no food. Also being gassed and killed in all sorts of ways. (Please do read books about Treblinka, Auschwitz, Bergen-Belsen, Dachau, and the other concentration camps).

So to speak, the U.S. Army treated us with kindness. Shivering in my shorts and knee socks, I was given a very small U.S. uniform and yet I still had to roll up the trousers, including very small army boots. I was asked a lot of questions about the army, the whereabouts of weapons, etc. I told them everything I knew. Strangely, I knew a lot, as we schoolboys had been working with the army for now over one year without any schooling.

I had not seen my Mum for days as the GIs and officers separated me from the villagers for fear they would kill me for having given away their hiding place. At the end of April all detainees in that church, including myself,

BORN ON THE WRONG SIDE OF THE FENCE

were put into Army trucks. Not having been told where we were being taken, it was to our surprise that 60 minutes later we were allowed to disembark. God in heavens, the destination was the entrance of the notorious Flossenburg concentration camp. The place of course some of us had never seen or known about. I was surrounded by hundreds of U.S. soldiers with their guns and rifles ready to shoot. We had to line up, two abreast, in a very long column. The U.S. Army also brought in hundreds of other people from surrounding villages and towns. Young boys and girls from the age of eight years were led by their Mums or grandparents. Children below the age of eight and pregnant women had to be separated and were led away to another section of the camp.

Entering this camp, which incidentally was liberated by the 90th Division and my friend Vern Schmidt the week before, brought on hysterical crying, sobbing and fainting to lots of those Germans forced here to visit. We were marched towards those huge open pits. Inside of them were hundreds upon hundreds of dead, decomposing bodies of Jewish and other nationalities including children and babies.

Although Flossenburg was not a major extermination camp in itself, these dead people had been brought there in the last days of the war as the U.S. and English/French armies were slowly advancing from west to east.

We were led through the room with the cremation ovens and the room with the stone table where bodies lay in a heap ready for whatever. We passed heaps and heaps of glasses, shoes, shirts, trousers, ladies' underwear and personal items. The prisoners had to strip before going to their death.

The smell of those rotting corpses was overbearing. Women fainted, and had to be dragged away by U.S. soldiers. Nobody was allowed to stop walking. The barracks where those unfortunate humans lived had to be burned to the ground as they were infected by typhus, lice, bugs, etc. The most horrible sight of all was an enormous heap of ashes and bones and a wall with thousands of bullet holes and the ground red with blood. My Mum screamed her head off as she demanded to know why in hell we young children had to see this slaughter. The answer was again by the U.S. lady officer, "So that your boys cannot say, in years to come, that it never happened."

Then it was over. We had to climb up on the trucks and be taken back 38 kilometers to Leuchtenburg to our church home. On the way back, no words were spoken. All of us were in shock. Men with staring eyes, thinking, "God, if we only knew." For years they were screaming their heads off with Heil Hitler, Heil Hitler, our beloved Fuhrer, whilst behind the scenes millions went to their death.

BORN ON THE WRONG SIDE OF THE FENCE

Finally we arrived back home at Leuchtenburg. One could have heard a needle drop. Men and women with their children disembarked with pale faces, and some had to be assisted to our temporary living quarters at the church; so terrible was the day's adventure for some of them.

The U.S. Army started to pack up, ready for their departure and advancement towards Austria. However, they left behind a skeleton team of U.S. administration and medical personnel in the German medical hospital next to our hotel.

Early the next morning the church bells started ringing, which was very unusual so early in the morning. We all knew that there was to be a special announcement and so it was. We all had to assemble in front of our church with our meager belongings. We had the feeling that our release was imminent as it had been now over three weeks in that confinement in the church.

Again, now our lovable U.S. lady officer bellowed in her broken German dialect this long awaited message. However good this new message was it hit us like a bombshell. "Ladies and Gentlemen of Leuchtenburg," she began. "Today you all can go home to your place of residence. The United States Army had U.S. soldiers and officers living in your homes. You can trust us. Nothing has been taken or stolen. However, some residences have been searched (baloney, most of us thought). But now to further good news. As most of you probably have known the castle and the chapel under the control of the SS and Gestapo were used as storing places of military equipment and clothing for the last two years. Also they contained personal belongings taken from murdered inmates of the Concentration Lager Flossenburg. Those items have been removed for further investigation and in some cases to be returned to surviving relatives or family members in the near future. However, all military clothing has been left for you all here in Leuchtenburg."

True to her words, the Castle chapel was later opened but without any type of U.S. control or organized handout. It was a total animalistic storm towards the Castle chapel, uphill about 600 meters. Old and young. Therefore the elderly and sick villagers never reached the place in time for the best choices. Military uniforms were taken to be retailored into suits and working clothes for men. They went so far as to recolor the dark green military uniforms into darker colors. God! It was so funny to see all those refits later in the village. Germany had no clothing industry left for years as the Allied bombing knocked all those factories out. Any sort of clothing or clothing material was unobtainable in the last three war years. But the first thing the villagers took were Army blankets, socks, boots, gloves, parachute material and

BORN ON THE WRONG SIDE OF THE FENCE

especially woolen socks and scarves. Military jackets lined with sheepskin for pilots of the Luftwaffe were all stored here while soldiers on the Russian front fighting in subzero temperatures froze to death. They lacked those life-giving items which had been rechanneled by corrupt Nazi Party members and officials during the last year of the war. On top of all this misery, hundreds, even thousands of inmates in the terrible concentration lagers froze to death in their wooden bunks for lack of warm clothing. There were stories of prisoners clinging together in the night in their bunks to transfer body heat and still freezing to death. While here some corrupt Nazis stored all these life-giving items in Leuchtenburg's castle. Tons of it! Hard to believe my friends. The more I think back the clearer it becomes.

I have returned in the late Eighties and Nineties to Leuchtenburg for further investigation; especially on this subject. I got very little response from the locals. I have asked the aged ones but nobody remembers anything!!! But here again history cannot be changed. Nazi officials siphoned these goods away for their own use, betraying their own soldiers and suffering German civilians. It was true; corrupt German Nazi Party members, high ranking officers, lower ranks in the Party – they well knew the war was over. We will look after ourselves first. Only one thing: They never estimated how quick and fast the glorious U.S. Army would advance to put an end to all those miserable deeds.

After the war hundreds of Nazi Party members committed suicide or fled to other countries to escape the punishment they greatly deserved. However, the German SS troops and Gestapo removed truckloads of those stored items moments before the liberation of Leuchtenburg which I myself and my brother observed. Moments before they left, they put me in one of their flatbed trucks and asked me to come with them. Me, a nine year old boy. What a joke! I had to jump out of the moving truck and hit the tar road so hard with my knees that it took all the top skin off. Today I often wonder what would have happened if I had stayed with them. God! It would have killed my Mum for sure. But even in those days I had this self-preservation mind, or an angel looking after me.

So rather than let the villagers, including my Mum, go home first, they made a gross mistake by opening the chapel first. Now they ran up to the castle, pushing and wrestling to be one of the first there. Again the strongest, most heavily built farmers' wives pushed my skinny mother away. She had no chance to be there first. Contrary to our belief that the Americans would issue those goods, no, this was not the case. They had separated all confiscated prisoners' belongings already and these had been taken away. Now the show was on. The villagers stormed the castle like animals. The door to the chapel is very small in comparison to a normal door because people 900 years ago were smaller than today, by nearly 20 centimeters. To get into that chapel and out with those items was like fighting a war, everyone grabbing what they could carry. It reminded me of animals like lions wrestling on a carcass. The screaming words of "Go away," "No, this is mine," "I got here first" echoed through the castle walls. My poor Mum arrived there late and all we found was two army blankets, one parachute and three pairs of officers' gloves. Everything else had been taken, cleaned out in one hour. The chapel was cleared of nearly 15 tons of goods.

The struggle was over. Exhausted, Mum, myself and my brother wobbled home down through the castle's gate and around the corner of the church where I had been captured weeks before, down to our hotel, our room, home for the last two years of misery. A new beginning.

Chapter 7

Homecoming

Walking home we again heard the church bell ringing. People whispered to each other quietly. I asked my mother, "What's the matter now?" and she whispered in my ear, "The war is over Bruno." It was the 9th of May, 1945.

Sometimes I remember the innocent question I asked. "Mum, who won the war?" She just grabbed me by the arm, tears running from her eyes, and whispered, "We lost. Just hope Dad's coming home." Having not seen Dad for over two years, Mum was on the verge of collapsing, which I sensed, even as a nine year old. Poor Mum not only had to put up with all of this misery, including my brother's asthma, but with not knowing if Dad was dead or alive.

This was only the beginning of our trouble. Arriving at the hotel, Mum looked up to our hole where the window was, now partly fixed with wooden boards.

We made our way up the staircase leading to our room, expecting it to be messed up and unlivable. We opened the door and to our surprise, it was spotlessly clean. Mum said to me alarmingly, "Bruno, our carpet is missing." Mum's carpet was a two- by three-meter Persian rug given to us by Aunty Rosa from Purkersdorf near Vienna. The carpet was nearly 50 years old then. Mum started crying and became really upset, looking onto the bare floorboards. Opening our only wardrobe, to our amazement, there was our carpet, standing nicely rolled up in the corner among Mum's dresses and blouses.

We dragged the carpet out of the wardrobe and started to roll it out. We then smelled it and it had the unmistakable stink of urine and excrement which were piled up in the middle of the carpet and then rolled up like a large pancake. Mum said nothing. She just rolled it up, dragged it out and put it on the cart. Then we pulled it out into the woods and buried it.

Coming home, we started to clean the floor and to our great, great surprise, the unbelievable thing, under the bed was (hold your breath, readers) a large U.S. food parcel. It was unopened and weighed at least six kilograms. First Mum did not know what it was, also thinking it could be another joke

BORN ON THE WRONG SIDE OF THE FENCE

like our carpet. No, it was not. God in heaven! Mum's tears were just rolling down her face. Her hands were shaking as she opened the parcel. First Mum locked the door and told us boys not to tell anyone. To our disbelief, there was chocolate, coffee, biscuits, tinned food, bully beef, cigarettes, medicines including condoms and much more. I cannot remember anymore but one thing I have never forgotten: my first bite into that chocolate and Mum's first taste for a long, long time of coffee. Wow!! We all just sat there all day in that room; we munched, ate and drank. There had to be more than one GI billeted in this our room. One of them must have been a witness to the bad behavior of his comrades. Feeling remorseful, he quickly slipped a good (U.S. rations) parcel under our bed. A man of God, I pray, and hope that this GI survived the war and I hope to find him one day and thank him for what he did. He may have had to go without this food, God only knows.

Regarding this incident, we never felt any animosity towards any of them. How could we for what they did? The brave young spirited U.S. GIs were our saviors, giving their blood and lives for us. A lot of us have forgotten by now, but I never shall. Today, having been in the permanent Royal Australian Air Force for 20 years and having experienced war and peace, I can understand why all this happened. The atrocities the German armies and also civilians did to all their prisoners and slave laborers, including captured GIs and other nations' soldiers, is the most inhuman thing one can do. These brought on terrible revenge to some of the German civilians. Some of those infantry soldiers must have seen some very terrible things in those parts of Germany. Especially the consequences of the Flossenburg camp death march towards the south. Thousands of dead prisoners were strewn amongst the ditches of the road, shot only because they could not drag their decimated frames any longer. With tears in their eyes, staring into an SS pistol, waiting, waiting for that shot. The one you never hear. Last pleas useless; last fleeting memories of home far away – wife, mum, kids. Sunken eyes staring in that cold winter's day. Tears. "Bang." The GIs found hundreds of them but to go too deeply into what I saw with my nine year old eyes would bring back nightmares. One can see what every U.S. infantryman went through day after day, giving their lives, souls and health to liberate us from the evil Hitler and his henchmen.

As the road of the death march was only one kilometer from us, and being little boys, knowing the woods with every nook and ditch, we followed the banging, shooting and yelling. We hid among the trees and bushes and my brother and I witnessed the slaughter in front of our eyes. Frozen with fear, we retreated. This scene is permanently embossed in my brain, especially one old

BORN ON THE WRONG SIDE OF THE FENCE

man's hand raised. The lost look on that blue cold winter's day. His spindly legs with no socks in his striped prisoner gear. At zero temperature, death was a relief from his agony. The prisoners marched on and every kilometer, one was slaughtered. God be with them. Fifty-eight years later, I found God. God was denied me as a young child but God does not forget you. Only by believing in Him, I have found peace in my mind and soul as we all will be resurrected one day and judged according to our sins.

Some religions were especially hounded by the German Nazis. The Jehovah's Witnesses in particular. The following is a story written by one of them, who survived the Holocaust. May this be a reminder to all of us. Let us not forget the nations that sent their young and brave to fight evil. I thank, on my knees, the brave heroic U.S. Army, especially the 90th Infantry Division, for our delivery from those terrible years of evil. I pray for their dead and all of the wounded, in body and spirit, those men and women who survived and their suffering families back home. To all of them, thanks from a little boy soldier.

Chapter 8

The Death March
(The following is the account of a survivor of the death march from Flossenburg)

By April 1945, the western Allies were pressing in on the Berlin area from the west and the Russians were advancing from the east. The Nazi leaders studied various means of liquidating the inmates of the concentration camps. But killing off hundreds of thousands of people and disposing of their bodies within a few days without leaving behind any trace of their heinous crimes proved to be too difficult for these fiendish men. So they decided to kill off the sick and march the rest to the nearest seaport where they would be loaded onto ships that would be taken out to sea and sunk, sending the prisoners to a watery grave.

From Sachsenhausen, we were due to march some 250 kilometers (155 miles) to Lubeck. Departure was scheduled for the night of April 20-21, 1945. The prisoners were first to be assembled by nationality. How thankful to Jehovah we were, therefore, when all Witness prisoners were ordered to assemble in the tailor shop! There were 230 of us, from six different countries. The Witnesses who were sick in the infirmary, occupants of which were to be killed before the evacuation, were saved by brothers at the risk of their lives and were carried to the tailor shop.

Indescribable confusion reigned among the other prisoners. Much stealing went on. As for us, we held an "assembly" and strengthened one another spiritually. Soon, however, our turn came to begin the long march, supposedly to a reassembly camp but actually to a planned watery death. The various nationalities left in groups of 600 prisoners – first the Czechs, then the Poles and so forth – some 26,000 in all. The group of Jehovah's Witnesses was the last to leave. The SS had given us a cart to haul. I learned later that it contained some of the loot the SS had plundered from among the prisoners. They knew Jehovah's Witnesses would take none of it.

That cart turned out to be a blessing because sick and elderly ones were able to sit on top and rest for a while during the march. When one got his strength back, he would get down and walk and another Witness, too weak to

BORN ON THE WRONG SIDE OF THE FENCE

follow, would take his place and so on, through the two weeks that the "death march" lasted. It was in every sense a "death march" because not only was our destination to be a watery grave but death lurked along the way. Anyone who could not keep up was mercilessly dispatched by an SS bullet. Some 10,700 were to lose their lives that way before the march ended. Yet, through Christian love and solidarity, not one Witness was left on the wayside to be killed by the SS.

The first 50 kilometers (30 miles) were a nightmare. The Russians were so near that we could hear the guns. Our SS taskmasters were afraid of falling into the hands of the Soviets, so that first lap, from Sachsenhausen to Neuruppin, turned out to be a forced march that lasted 36 hours.

I had started out carrying a few meager belongings but upon getting more and more tired, I threw away one thing after another until nothing was left but a blanket in which to roll up at night. Most nights we slept outdoors, with just twigs and leaves to keep us from the damp ground. One night, however, I was able to sleep in a barn. Imagine my surprise to find a Vindication book (a Watchtower publication) hidden in the straw! The following morning our hosts gave us something to eat. But that was exceptional. After that, for days on end we had nothing to eat or drink except for a few plants we were able to obtain and use to make herb tea at night, when we stopped to sleep. I remember seeing some non-Witness prisoners rush over to the carcass of a horse that had been killed near the road and devour the flesh in spite of the blows of their SS guards who hit them with their rifle butts.

All this time, the Russians were advancing on one side and the Americans on the other. By April 25, the situation was so confused that our SS guards no longer knew where the Soviets or the U.S. troops were so they ordered the whole column of prisoners to camp in a wooded area for four days. While there, we ate nettles, roots and tree bark. This delay proved to be providential for had they kept us marching, we would have reached Lubeck before the German army collapsed and would have ended up at the bottom of Lubeck Bay.

The Last Night

On April 29, the SS decided to move the prisoners on toward Lubeck. They hoped to get us there before the Russian and American forces joined up. The march continued for several days and by that time we were approaching Schwerin, a city located some 50 kilometers from Lubeck. Once again the SS ordered us to hide in the woods. It turned out to be our last night in captivity. But what a night!

BORN ON THE WRONG SIDE OF THE FENCE

The Russians and the Americans were closing in on the remnants of the German forces and shells were whistling over our heads from both sides. An SS officer advised us to walk on unguarded to the American lines, about six kilometers away, but we were suspicious of this. We prayed to Jehovah for guidance and we finally decided to spend the night in the woods. We later learned that those prisoners who had accepted this officer's proposal and had tried to get through to the American lines had been shot down by the SS. About 1,000 of them died that night. How thankful we were for Jehovah's protection!

However, that last night in Crivitz Wood was anything but peaceful. As the fighting grew nearer, our SS guards got panicky. Some of them slipped away into the night while others hid their weapons and uniforms, donning the striped garb taken from dead prisoners. Those who were recognized were shot by prisoners who had found the weapons left behind. The confusion was indescribable! Men were running hither and thither and bullets and shells were flying everywhere. But we Witnesses kept together and weathered the storm under Jehovah's protecting hand, until the next morning. We expressed our gratitude to Jehovah in a Resolution adopted on May 3, 1945. We had marched some 200 kilometers in 12 days. Of the 26,000 prisoners who left the Sachsenhausen concentration camp on that "death march," barely more than 15,000 survived. Yet every last one of the 230 Witnesses who had left the camp came through that ordeal alive. What a wonderful deliverance!

On May 5, 1945, I made contact with the American forces and on May 21, I arrived back home in Harnes, northern France. I had survived the death march and certainly shared David's feelings, expressed in Psalm 23:4, "Even though I walk in the valley of deep shadow, I fear nothing bad, for you are with me; your rod and your staff are the things that comfort me."

The death march from Sachsenhausen proved to be just one lap in the journey through the present system of things on toward the goal of life. Many have been my joys in sharing the "good news" since that time. Even as Jehovah has allowed me to survive that terrible march, my prayer is that, with my wife and three children, I will keep on walking on the narrow road of life, avoiding pitfalls to the right and to the left. Matt. 7:134, 14: Isa. 30:20,21.

(Here the death march survivor's story ends. From 11,000 emaciated prisoners who left KZ Flossenburg on the Death March south, 6,000 survived, thanks to the 90th Division, which evacuated hundreds to makeshift military hospitals.)

Chapter 9

Dad's Capture (as told by my father)

My father's days as a fighting man in his Tiger tank came to an end in Hungary. They were retreating from the advancing Russians and finally in winter 1945 had to abandon their tanks as the supply of petrol and ammunition came to an abrupt halt. Part of Dad's 13th Division was cut off. His order was to disband, everyone for himself. The tanks were scuttled and blown up. So Dad and four of his crew traveled only by night and from farm to farm, hiding during the day. Capture by the now advancing Russians meant instant execution or exile to Siberia. So they limited contact with civilians altogether, for fear someone may dob them in, as happened to many Germans who asked civilians for help.

After many days traveling and living from handouts given by friendly farmers, they reached the Czech border, their motto – "little as possible contact with the civilian population." For days they traveled by night along the border toward Germany, as Dad knew Mum and us kids were there. But one of his mates left them, crossing into eastern Austria, which saved his life. One night they crawled into an abandoned saw mill to have a few hours of sleep. The sawdust was so inviting they just dropped onto the heaps and fell asleep. Early in the morning noises from an approaching troop of men woke them up, but as those men were so close escape was fruitless. So they dug themselves into the mountains of sawdust and covered themselves completely.

Unfortunately, one of them had his boot sticking out of the sawdust and that was his death sentence. Those timber workers started up the band saw to do a day's work. One of them discovered the unfortunate German soldier's boot sticking out of the sawdust. He grabbed him and dragged the German, screaming, towards the band saw. That's when my father's self-preservation instinct cut in. Yelling to his other two mates, they made a dash out of the sawdust towards the open door, past the stunned workers and out of the sawmill towards the river, running along the sawmill. Dad told me the last thing he saw was his comrade being sliced in two by the band saw. A horror

BORN ON THE WRONG SIDE OF THE FENCE

which in later years cost my Dad many nightmares and sleepless nights. I will describe this in the following chapters.

Running toward the river and followed by an angry mob of Czech mill workers, they started to wade across the thankfully low running stream of water. Then, in the hail of bullets, one of his mates was hit in the back and tumbled head first into the stream. The remaining comrade received a hit in the buttocks. With my father's help he made it across, thankful to be alive. Incredibly, the mill workers did not follow them across the river.

At that time, my father did not know that this river was the border between western Austria and Czechoslovakia. Safely across and hopeful for a now safe journey, this idea was cut short, as out of the morning mist and out of nowhere, Dad and his mate found themselves surrounded by dozens of American GIs who, of course, took them as prisoners, but gently looked after Dad's wounded comrade. Relieved by the Americans' kindness, Dad's war was over. The 90th Division took care of them. They were transported to a holding camp not far from the Czech border in eastern Bavaria, somewhere near Weiden or Cham. Incidentally, the 90th Division was the same Division which captured me.

Arriving at the U.S. Army holding camp, Dad was interrogated and happily they accepted Dad's story, and being a mechanical engineer, he was given a job in the repair shop fixing damaged military vehicles, especially tanks, which of course gave him a better style of everyday life in the camp. Most German prisoners never experienced this. He worked hard and it had its rewards; extra smokes, extra food and extra medicines which he shared with his comrades.

Hundreds of German soldiers were living in that camp from May to June of 1945. The U.S. military had nothing for them to do, so they invented this time-absorbing job – the German prisoners had to sit by tables and everyone received two house bricks and one hammer; then they passed boxes of four-inch nails around. To the sound of Mozart and Beethoven blaring out of huge loudspeakers hanging from a post, they had to bend one nail between two bricks, then pass that bent nail to the next prisoner who had to straighten it out. That nail was then passed on to the next for bending again, and so on.

In later years when Dad told me this story, everybody laughed themselves sick, but at that time in the camp, no one was allowed to laugh. It was a deadly serious affair.

One day in May 1945, the U.S. camp commander opened the gate of the prison. Everybody was issued a box of supplies and five American dollars.

BORN ON THE WRONG SIDE OF THE FENCE

They said everybody in the camp was to go home to wherever they came from, as by then they had separated the Germans who had committed war crimes and shipped them to prisons in Berlin or Nuremberg to be tried. Astonishingly, before leaving, Dad was asked by his superior U.S. officer if he would like to stay with them in the U.S. Army and was even invited to take the whole family to the United States in the later months. Unfortunately, Dad declined but many German technicians and academics took up this invitation just as the rocket scientist Werner von Braun did. So, like the other hundreds of prisoners, he decided to go home.

Dad was thankful to the U.S. military and especially to the 90th Division for treating him so well. Had he been captured by the Russians or Czech or Polish partisans, his life would not have been worth a nickel. So the doors opened, the camp was vacated, and they all thanked the U.S. commander and his troops, the 90th Division, and they went home. Very sadly, some to a very disappointing ending.

Chapter 10

Days of Liberation

Slowly the insanity of war was replaced with the mad chaos of rebuilding a totally destroyed nation. We in the country had it a little bit better than our cousins in the city. We could gather food from the forest including all the firewood for cooking and heating which of course city dwellers were not able to do. Also we had the benefit of having been surrounded by farmers.

For a few weeks we totally relied on the food given to us by the Red Cross and other charities. The food was fresh and wholesome. Mum now was known in our district for her beautiful hand-made dolls. She spent hours on her sewing machine creating never-ending different models of dolls including dresses. Later she painted their little faces with colored pencils and the whole dolls were stuffed with sawdust. The end product was a simple 12-inch doll loved by all the girls around here and very popular with farm children. Commercial children's toys in the postwar months were nonexistent. Mum had no trouble feeding us boys. Today I laugh when I think of my first suit which was made by her out of an army blanket rescued from the castle chapel.

After we were released from our temporary holding camps and returned home, school resumed a few days later. It was a sad homecoming to our school. The building was totally ravaged by the fleeing German army. Sadly also it was stripped bare by looters and all that was left was our stove and nearly all our benches and the blackboard. The first two days were spent cleaning up the mess and then we received our first books with all the Nazi symbols cut out. Oh yes, that pathetic Hitler picture above the blackboard was now ceremoniously burned in our woodstove. The best was no more morning parades and Hitler songs.

Then, shortly after the liberation of Leuchtenburg, the whole population of our village experienced this hilarious incident. Six weeks after Easter a Corpus Christi ceremony is held commemorating the triumphal entry of Jesus into Jerusalem. Therefore our main street through the village, which is only wide enough to let a Sherman tank through without scratching the sides of the buildings on both sides, was covered the day before with nearly eight inches of

BORN ON THE WRONG SIDE OF THE FENCE

freshly cut grass and mixed with flowers. The road on both sides was decorated with freshly cut birch tree branches and flowers. This highly decorated street led right up to our church. The distance from the entrance of our village to the church was about 500 meters. The celebration started at this point, so on this very day early in the morning, two separate groups of people were preparing for the day ahead. First, the village priest with hundreds of highly dressed up Germans in folk costumes; small children in their best outfits, and all the little girls in their white dresses with flower garlands in their hair. Then there were the floats. The whole idea was and it still is today as it was hundreds of years ago, that this procession follows the priest and a man sitting on a donkey acting as Jesus Christ entering Jerusalem over this grassy carpet up to the church. This was followed by a very special service. Not only do these highly dressed up village people march over the grass, there are hundreds more coming from miles around to witness this special event.

The same day, exactly at the same time, early in the morning, another party was getting ready to enter our village, not to occupy it but just to pass through on the way to Vohenstraus ten kilometers to the east. First we heard the rumble far away, then as it came nearer and nearer we all started listening and worrying, "What could it be?" To our amazement, approaching around the corner of our street and coming to an abrupt halt, was a huge, dirty Sherman tank, fully laden with GIs hanging from every point. It was followed by several jeeps, trucks, artillery and lots of infantry. I remember hanging out of our now repaired window, wondering what the hell they are doing here as the main road was only one kilometer away going in the same direction.

By now a lot of people had gathered around this convoy. It didn't take long for a high ranking officer to approach this gathering group. With his unmistakably Yankee smile and a Camel hanging out of his mouth, he asked to speak to the newly elected Burgermeister. The conversation lasted about 15 minutes, a long, long time for a highly vulnerable military convoy to sit there; although Germany had surrendered, there still were a lot of fanatic Nazis who took potshots at the moving troops, causing a lot of fatalities in the month to follow.

The comical scene that followed was like something out of a movie. The Burgermeister rushed up to the waiting convoy and approached this officer in this funny looking periodic Bavarian outfit. Not being outgunned by this GI officer, he put on a bright pearly smile and extended his right hand to greet this somehow nervous GI. So there they were standing in the middle of the road, the mayor standing about one foot from the beginning of the grassy road

BORN ON THE WRONG SIDE OF THE FENCE

and the officer about one meter away from this tank. The conversation was as follows.

U.S. OFFICER: Please Sir, remove the grass!

MAYOR: I can't do that. The procession is to start in five minutes.

U.S. OFFICER: I can't take any chances to drive over your grass. There may be mines underneath. Okay?

MAYOR (laughing): Sir, we did not know you were coming. But MINES?

U.S. OFFICER: Okay, Buddy. You guys do your procession and we'll follow.

MAYOR: That's okay with me.

U.S. OFFICER (to his troops): Take five.

So the Mayor lined up this religious Corpus Christi procession and they all took off. Drums and trumpets and singing, following the "standing Jesus" on his donkey, the priest and all the villagers. Followed by a Sherman tank, jeeps, trucks, infantry and artillery. The aftermath of all that traffic was a mish mash of pulped grass and flowers. Today, thinking of that day makes me cry and laugh all at the same time.

The moral of this story is that the officer in charge of this convoy stopped the troops after clearing the grass and urged some of his troops to join us in the service in our church. Many did and others enjoyed the hour's rest. I hope that someday this story will shake someone's memory. I hope it will be a GI from the 90th Division.

Chapter 11

My Friends the GIs of the 90th Division

Days after this humorous incident, more troops arrived and some of them moved into our hotel, "Gasthof zum Burgkrug." Most of them were administration officers, drivers and security staff including MPs. Their headquarters were in Weiden about 24 kilometers from Leuchtenburg, and some of them traveled from there every day. Also a lot of equipment was shipped here from Weiden.

The young Bavarian ladies just loved those ever-smiling Yanks as they were called. It had something to do with those nylon stockings they offered them in large quantities. How they got hold of them so fast during the days of the war will be a mystery to me forever. We boys saw a lot of our young frauleins kissing and cuddling some lucky GI and it was very common in later months that the birthrate went up a little here in Leuchtenburg. Later, as I grew up and understood more about the birds and the bees, I could not blame either of them, the frauleins or the GIs.

The frauleins had never seen so much attention ever, as most young German men had been drafted into the army and there was the factor that the U.S. GIs had a lot of "goodies" such as nylon stockings, chocolate, cigarettes, perfumes, coffee, etc., which of course the frauleins loved and, in the hard days following the surrender, those goodies were used to barter for more essential goods. The poor GIs had not only risked their lives every day and never knew if they would survive another day, so they used every opportunity to have a little loving and cuddling. How could anybody deny it to them? Later we saw many of those young ladies marry their GI sweethearts and move with them to the U.S.

I may add here that it happened not only to the GIs, but I saw it happen to other soldiers like Russians, French and especially English soldiers. A young lady by the name of Julie Wimmer had her hand blown off by playing with a hand grenade she found in the vineyard, married a Russian Mongolian soldier by whom she got pregnant and in 1952 went with him to Mongolia; a happy outcome. I must say here that of course many pregnant girls were left with

BORN ON THE WRONG SIDE OF THE FENCE

their babies forever, as this also happened in the Vietnam War. Had Julie Wimmer been stuck with her Mongolian looking baby by herself, it would have had bad consequences for her. We could see this in later years when there were babies fathered to Vietnam girls who had a very different facial appearance and stood out in the crowd and therefore had terrible times in their young lives.

Now I became again popular with the GIs as they remembered that I was captured just outside of the castle walls and had worked with the German troops as a temporary runner, loader, etc. They asked me one day if I knew where some or all of the remaining telephone wires and radio equipment was, as some of it was still in the top of the castle tower and the remaining cut wires were still dangling down from it. So I told them that in the last days, just before I had been ordered to that gun crew, I had worked in the attic of the German communication center just outside of the castle, unrolling those cables and dragging them up there with some of my school comrades. Therefore I had seen all this radio and transmitting equipment up there. I had no idea what it was as at nine years of age; all this made no sense to me. I just did what they told me to do. As mentioned before, the Germans had an observation post up there. The GIs then took me up to the house on the right hand side of the castle wall gate and the church, climbing up to the attic and forcing open the only door. There they found tons of smashed up radio and telephone equipment including those wires they were looking for. All I remember are the words they said, "God damn, it's all here." I received a pat on my shoulder and chewing gum. They thanked me for my help and Mum received a very nice K-ration parcel that evening and we were instructed not to tell anyone of all of this.

Chapter 12

Dad's Return

Three more months slipped by and it was now May-June 1945. We got used to the U.S. Army and they got used to us and life started to be near normal again. The occupying U.S. forces helped the German civilians to such an extent that one month after this great war, life was getting back on track. Here I must say again, over and over, that especially in Leuchtenburg the 90th Division, known under the name of "The Tough Ombres," did their utmost to help our starving and elderly people. Not only did we receive enough food, we also were looked after medically and health wise.

School started again but otherwise we still went out in the woods to collect the firewood and mushrooms and berries, including as many stinging nettles and herbs for tea as we could find. So many lovely fruits and food Mother Nature supplied for us. I thank God for all of this. At today's standard of living, hardly anyone takes the trouble to go out in the woods to collect those free and healthy foods Mother Nature supplies for us.

One day Mum was munching on a bit of dry bread crust from our meager U.S. food rations. Starting down to the steep descending street opposite our house, she suddenly collapsed on the floor. Lying there and with her bread still between her lips, she mumbled, "Your Father, your Father is coming!" I rushed to her assistance and my little brother jumped down from the kitchen chair in excitement and we both tried to sit Mum up, which of course was an easy task for us as Mum was by now after six years of war a very, very skinny lady.

Moments later the door to our room opened up and there in the semidarkness stood this unshaven, really dirty man, in a half German and half U.S. uniform, rushing up to Mum and us. Until today I don't know why on earth we boys just took off. We bolted past this man and out of our room, down the stairs and into the beer garden. We just sat on one of those beer garden benches and waited and waited until Mum came down to assure us that this really gross looking man was our Dad we hadn't seen for so long. She ushered us upstairs and we now saw a clean-shaven, neatly dressed man sitting

BORN ON THE WRONG SIDE OF THE FENCE

on one of our kitchen chairs, staring at us. He never said a word. It must have been very hard for him. So many years of not having seen his boys he only dreamed about in the trenches of Russia.

We boys just stood there. Was it reality? Was it our Dad? The Dad we had heard of, day after day? Deep, deep down our conscience took over and we slowly approached our Dad. The Dad we longed for so long. He touched us gently and we received each a bag of chocolate and sweets he had saved from his camp rations. The ice was broken. It must have been totally and emotionally devastating for him.

Mum just cried for days as I can remember, and that night we slept in the barn on sweet-smelling freshly cut grass and straw. Mum and Dad had to do something to create in our small room more sleeping space. Dad now received from the Red Cross two army stretchers. They went side by side for our parents. Dad constructed out of secondhand timber double bunk beds for us boys. Dad assured us that in the very near future we would go back home to Austria to our beloved Purkersdorf in the lovely Vienna Woods. Home to our own family we had not seen for so long.

As springtime slowly changed to summer there was a mood change of the Bavarian people towards Austrians which intensified week by week. I could see it all around me. The native village people stopped talking to us and Dad and Mum realized that there was something going on, we just could not put our finger on it. My school friends and buddies of years stopped coming to play. Mum told us that the villagers also stopped talking to her. Then one day in late August 1945 the village priest came to see Mum and Dad. The news he gave us was something they never expected to happen. He warned my parents that in the very near future we would have to leave our beloved Leuchtenburg, our new home now for many years, especially for us children. I loved Leuchtenburg; the castle, the forest and brooks; even the Bavarian people I had started to love. However, this friendship was going to cease very soon, as again the people of Bavaria were stirred up by politics of their own doing. The reason behind all this at that time was very simple. Hitler was an Austrian, and so were we; my mother, my father, myself and my little brother. And as Hitler and Germany including Bavaria had lost the war, which brought untold misery and death to millions, we the migrated Austrians ("blow-ins") now were prosecuted for all that misery Hitler had brought unto them. A thousand homeless refugees from the eastern frontiers streamed into Germany and Bavaria, and we the Austrians were told to go where we bloody came from, and these were only some of the words they used.

BORN ON THE WRONG SIDE OF THE FENCE

Early in November it all came to a head. The children in school started to call me and my brother "Ostmark Schwein." Suddenly all our friends turned into enemies. On the street and everywhere we were called Ostmark Schwein, or "bloody go home you Ostmark Schwein." Mum started to cry and Dad started to have nightmares, reflections of battlefield incidents. Life was going to be hell in our little room in that hotel.

One day Dad was told to go see the Burgermeister of Leuchtenburg. There he was told that he had 24 hours to leave Bavaria and to return to Austria. Our German citizenship had been canceled and in this instant we were declared refugees. Dad was devastated. All we had was in one room, and most of it was junk.

With winter approaching fast and with Mum pregnant by now, we were afraid she would have a mental breakdown. In those days after the war with thousands of refugees seeking help, very little was obtainable. So with only one day to go, Dad gave notice to his boss. He loaded up our hand-drawn cart for our trip. Our trip home started in December 1945.

Terrible winds started coming from the east accompanied by ice and sleet. The roads were iced up and slippery. In this condition, Dad dragged our little cart with my brother totally covered with bedding towards our first destination, the little town of Vohenstraus, 12 kilometers from Leuchtenburg. Mum and I, covered in heavy winter clothing, helped Dad by pushing the little cart. Initially, the first kilometer out of Leuchtenburg was very steep. However, after leaving the village itself, the road leveled out so the pushing and pulling of the cart became a little easier. Slowly our little village started to fade away in the cold foggy winter's day; glimpses of the castle tower sticking out of the fog, and then the village was out of sight. This is still embedded in my memory today 60 years later. It took 50 years to come back to visit, only to see a different, modern town. The only things that had not changed were the castle and the woods.

Nevertheless, back to our trip. We entered the dark forest between Leuchtenburg and Vohenstraus. Reminders of the fighting between the American forces and the Germans were everywhere: burned out vehicles, tossed uniforms and hastily made graves indicated a fanatic resistance of the Wehrmacht. Believe me, walking through this was like a nightmare and having seen this since I was four years old, and with nine year olds having experienced fighting, this had not made a major impact on me.

Dad stopped the cart and reminded me of an incident I had forgotten long ago. He must have had this story told by my uncle who visited us just

BORN ON THE WRONG SIDE OF THE FENCE

after he came back from the camp earlier in the year, quite hilarious and it went like this; no wonder we lost the war! Early in 1944 my Uncle Walter, a Stuka pilot, came to visit us in Leuchtenburg. He looked very charming in his officer's uniform with his cap cheerfully pushed back on his head. On his black army belt hung an army issue Luger in a shiny leather holster. We kids loved Uncle Walter. He was funny and adored us children. "Uncle Walter," I said, "I am now helping in school with the loading of ammunition belts and learning to shoot, and helping with digging trenches and in general helping the SS around the castle." He was very impressed with my work and admired all the badges I had acquired during the last two years. So I asked Uncle Walter if he would be so kind as to let me have a go with the Luger. Well, Mum flew up in a rage but Uncle Walter said "Of course, Bruno, let's go out in the woods and I will let you have a shot." Toward Vohenstraus we marched. I was so proud of my uncle as all the villagers looked at him in his flashy uniform.

Approaching the Black Forest, we walked straight up to a large pine tree where Uncle Walter drew his Luger out of the holster. He passed it up to me and carefully pointed the weapon toward the tree. Pulling back the slide, he told me to pull the trigger. Well, BANG went the weapon. My hand flew up in the air and the rancid smell of burned cordite floated around in the still morning air. Pointing towards the tree, I noticed the white exposed timber of the pine tree, which reminded me now 50 years later of the bullet which missed my brother in the trench and hit the tree. Anyhow, I was so excited about that I asked Uncle Walter if I could have another go. My request was denied, and I was satisfied and thanked him for this experience.

Now to the conclusion of this story. Weeks later the Gestapo knocked on our door, with half the villagers looking on. They had Uncle Walter between them and he looked very upset. The Gestapo asked me if the story my uncle had told them was correct and told me that I would have to accompany them to that tree in the woods to find the spent cartridge to certify his story about him letting me shoot. Confirming this was true, we walked again out towards Vohenstraus. My uncle did not look well at all. He was pale and sweating, hoping to Jesus Christ we would find the cartridge in that moss-covered ground. Upon reaching the forest it didn't take me very long to find the tree and after searching for nearly 15 minutes we recovered a nice shining 9-millimeter Luger shell, and we had to dig the lead slug out of the tree on top of it. I today cannot remember much of this but Dad told me that German officers on leave took with them one clip of ammunition with their weapon, in this case a nine-bullet clip, and it had to be used ONLY in self-defense,

BORN ON THE WRONG SIDE OF THE FENCE

nothing else. Upon coming back from leave, Uncle Walter of course had only eight bullets and no alibi of any self-defense. In other words a German military command not obeyed. Had we not found this shell and the projectile, Uncle Walter would have had a very severe punishment.

In the last year of the war, millions died fighting the Americans, Russians, English and French on German soil, where thousands upon thousands of tons of ammunition was wasted, towns lay in rubble like my beloved Magdeburg or Vienna just two of many. The bloody GESTAPO worried and spent days chasing one lousy bullet. I always say, "No wonder they lost the war," ha ha, and Thank, God for that!!!

So past this military wrecking yard we trudged, my little brother Fritz now crying as the cold morning air brought on his never-ending asthma attacks and of all the wrong places, out there in the woods. But Mum carried with her some glass container and I cannot remember anymore how it worked but Fritz got slightly better.

Hours later we could see the town of Vohenstraus approaching. Not soon enough as Mum started to wobble on her legs. It was just too much for her and being in the early stages of pregnancy, the conditions we were exposed to took their toll. My father spotted a farmyard about half a kilometer from the road. He left us standing on the road and walked over to the main building only to discover it had been vacated and heavily damaged, presumably during combat. We pulled our cart over to the farm building again past foxholes and burned and damaged military equipment. Another reminder of what went on here months ago. Dad decided not to enter the main building as he later told me it could have been boobytrapped by some fanatic SS men. I was glad that my father had all that military experience necessary to survive out here. We all made ourselves at home in a large barn with lots of straw. Dad went out and organized the water and food. When he came back Mum was already asleep. Fritz and I had some meager food of herbal tea and dry bread with salt strewn over it and each an apple. Hardly had we gone to sleep in this very moldy smelling straw when Dad woke us up and told us that it was time to go. Mum had a nice hot cup of tea and some food my father had especially taken with us for her in her condition.

Tired and stiff, we arrived in Vohenstraus. This town was used by the 90th Division. We could see many U.S. soldiers walking about and cruising around in their jeeps. Vohenstraus is on the main route south towards Austria. Dad arranged with the Burgermeister and the Red Cross for passage to the city of Passau in a military bus supplied by the Red Cross to ferry certain refugees (like women, children and invalids). Passau was the nearest place for us to catch the train to Vienna, Austria.

In Vohenstraus we left our faithful cart and changed it for a nice but hard wooden bus seat, better than walking. The journey took us past some grizzly sights. Along the road we passed hundreds of open gravesites. We could see Germans under GI guards excavating many murdered prisoners' bodies hastily buried there months before by the fleeing German SS. Those were the unfortunates from the Flossenburg Concentration Lager on their death march towards Austria's death camps. Lucky for some of them they were rescued by the fast-overtaking U.S. forces before reaching their intended destination. Later in the night we arrived via the city of Cham at the lovely border town between Austria and Germany, Passau, in the province of Bavaria.

Again we had to sleep on straw but this time it was nice and new. The Red Cross supplied some hot beverage and food and we all slept like babies this night, as the next morning should bring to us the feeling that the poor Jews must have felt on their transport to the death camps. Except our transport was to freedom.

Chapter 13

The Trip Home

Mum was sick and pregnant. The trip from Leuchtenburg, the cold, the food, the worry, brought a serious case of diarrhea. Mum was exhausted and dehydrated as she lay moaning on a heap of straw. Dad had to call the camp doctor, a U.S. soldier, and a Red Cross sister. All they had was this black charcoal powder and black tea. Somehow Mum felt a little better and Dad relaxed a bit. He was so tired of dragging Mum to the toilet so many times, and all the cleaning up afterwards.

We young boys roamed around the camp all day annoying the GIs, begging for chocolate, cigarettes or chewing gum for trading. To our surprise, a lot of the GIs did respond to our begging and gave us some of their rations. But the girls had it better, especially the older ones. Well, that's life.

After many days of waiting we noticed that a huge amount of railroad boxcars were being shunted around and coupled together and some of them had rows of bullet holes in them. The stench of dead human bodies was everywhere and I did not realize at that time that much of that rolling stock was used to transport war prisoners and Jews to and from the Concentration Lagers. This rolling stock was also used for soldiers' transport to and from the eastern front.

The wagons had no toilet or water supply. Some had a large hole in the floor to use as the only manner to eject human waste. Some of the wagons were so shot up that it's a miracle they were still used for transport. Dad told me in later years that some of those wagons had bloated bodies in them for weeks before anybody had the opportunity to remove them; therefore that terrible smell. The U.S. ordered some of the camp refugees to clean the boxcars and all of them had about 12 inches of new straw put in. More and more refugees arrived at the holding camp in Passau and we noticed that most wagons had destinations painted on them like Vienna, Graz, Innsbruck, Linz, Budapest, etc. So departure was near.

Mum felt a little better but she had lost a few kilos in weight. Only the hot barley soup with meat we received every day saved my mother from having a miscarriage. We still thank the Red Cross today after sixty years for looking after my mother at that time of need.

BORN ON THE WRONG SIDE OF THE FENCE

One day we were given tags to attach to our clothing and after showering we were covered in DDT and told to report to our boxcar with our meager belongings. Hundreds upon hundreds of refugees stood there for hours in front of our boxcars and finally, after receiving a Red Cross food parcel each, we were told to enter our wagon. Just to climb up was a huge task for us and Mum in her condition as it was nearly four feet off the ground. Fifty persons per car and one forty gallon drum of water, and that hole in the corner. Luckily for us we had a reasonably solid carriage, but it had no windows. Two huge steam locomotives were coupled up, which nearly threw all of us into the straw as they connected, and after two long weeks of processing we finally left Passau for the long trek home to Vienna.

Slowly the train rumbled over the hills and down into the Danube valley. Today, a modern high speed train would only take five to six hours from Passau to Vienna, but our trip lasted days. There were many stops, some of them nearly a day long, where we had the opportunity to climb out of the wagons, stretch our legs or take a very short stroll, making sure not to stray too far from the train just in case they decided to pull away suddenly.

As we traveled through the early frosty winter days, the temperature in our wagon dropped to nearly zero degrees. After a few days traveling with no showers, the inside of the carriage started to smell. Say for instance, a lady wanted to go to the toilet (the hole in the floor). She had to ask someone in the carriage to hold a blanket up for her so she would have some privacy from all those prying eyes. But believe me, no one bothered, as most of us just sat or lay on the now trampled down straw.

The crying of the babies due to all this noise and the lack of proper food nearly drove us up the wall. Those poor mums. After a few days someone suggested to open the roller door to suck some fresh air into our carriage. However, to add to our misery the hot ashes from the steam engine got sucked through the open door into the wagon and nearly started a fire in our straw. Well, that was the end of having the door open. Fresh air was channeled into the carriage by some ingenious rotating devices on the top of the carriage roof. One day – and thanks to God it happened during the day and thanks to the engineer for seeing this which saved a massive loss of lives – as it happened, one of those unserviced rail wagons seized an axle bearing. It was due to not having any grease or oil in the bearing box. The result was a fire starting underneath the carriage's wooden floor and with the draft pushing the smoke into the carriage it started to suffocate the people inside. They all screamed in terror and opened the roller door which of course made it worse as it sucked

BORN ON THE WRONG SIDE OF THE FENCE

all the smoke inside. Slowly the train came to a halt, the engineers uncoupled the wagon; then the train pulled away a few yards and then uncoupled it again so it stood there by itself. All the people were evacuated from this carriage and they were looked after by a very friendly farmer nearby.

We were there for most of the day and the U.S. Army was bringing supplies to us, coffee and biscuits, apples, milk and bread. There we sat in the middle of Austria in early winter waiting for a rescue team to arrive. The U.S. Army toppled the carriage off the track. All persons were distributed into the already full wagons, then we were coupled up and away we went.

The next day we stopped at St. Poelten to fill up with water and coal and to offload some of the families and individuals. It took quite a while so some of us decided to take a stroll. So out we climbed from our wagon to cross a few rail tracks they used for shunting. My little brother started to cross by himself, without waiting for me, Dad or Mum to assist him. Very quietly and silently a rail wagon which was shunted around came rolling towards my brother. I yelled "Fritz, watch out!" He panicked and instead of jumping over the rails and out of harm's way he put his foot onto the icy cold slippery rail track and fell on his head between the rails. Mum screamed as the carriage rolled over my little brother. People came from all over the railyard running to give us some help. God must have looked after my little brother as the wagon just rolled over him. Because he was unconscious and not moving, he came into no contact with the rolling stock and all he needed was seven stitches on his eyebrow and a few hours' rest in the medical wagon looked after by a U.S. military nurse. All my life I've remembered this incident and when I see my brother we joke about this very serious incident.

One day there was a suicide in one of the wagons. A man cut his wrist in the night and not only killed himself but turned all of the mushy straw in the wagon blood red. Nobody could change it and all those poor people had to put up with it until Vienna, including the body.

Later that day the train stopped again as the tracks had to be repaired. A bomb crater which was close to the rail tracks had made the earth collapse and the rails were very badly buckled. Again this happened during the day. One could only imagine if this would have happened during the night. I have seen a train disaster, as described in an earlier chapter, and I thank God for having spared us from a very serious derailment.

Closer and closer we approached to Vienna and the country outside looked more and more like a war zone. Most villages sort of clustered around the railway system. The bombing by the Allied air forces, which tried very

BORN ON THE WRONG SIDE OF THE FENCE

hard to knock them out to stop movements of German troops, also leveled a lot of those towns and cities. It looked terrible to us and rumor had it that Vienna was also 90 percent bombed out.

The next day, after many days of traveling, we approached Vienna. All along the railway track everything was bombed and blown up. Cars, tanks, houses, factories, bridges and churches were absolutely unbelievable. Mum just cried for hours as did most of the people on the train. Where was Hitler now with his great generals and his great ideas? As we rolled into the lovely Vienna woods, the villages well known to me were all in ruins. Two kilometers outside our final destination, Vienna's Westbahnhof (Main West Railway Station) was also the end of the western railway system. Everything was bombed out, burned out, caved in. Molten glass and melted steel bridges. What happened to all those people who lived in all those houses, thousands upon thousands? God help us. Poor Mum and Dad and us children had no idea of what was in store for us. As we had had no contact with any of our family and relations for months, we did not know if our families were alive, or if their homes were still standing.

Finally, after many days of terror on the train, we came to a standstill in this burned out shell of one of Europe's biggest railway stations. We were surrounded by French Army nurses, doctors and first aid people from the Red Cross. Mum was helped out and put on a stretcher to be looked after by a very friendly French doctor. Why French, you may say. Well, we happened to be in the French zone. Vienna was divided into four military sectors. American, French, English and Russian. So we all stood there; Dad, Fritz, myself and Mum on a stretcher. We each received a large box of rations and then we were given our first Austrian registration card. We were now ready to start our new, free life in our homeland.

The horror which unfolded before my eyes was indescribable. What I had seen years earlier, when part of Magdeburg was bombed and burned, was only a minor incident against what happened in Vienna. Vienna was laid in total ruin. Streets kilometers long were lined on both sides with burned out and collapsed buildings. Glass mixed with bricks and mortar, concrete and warped steel beams meters high filled ninety percent of all roads. Streets usually twenty or more meters wide had only a three-foot path winding through the rubble. Tramlines that were ripped up and used for the last street defenses lay rusting mixed up with rubble. Burned out car and truck bodies were everywhere. Military hardware, German, Russian, etc., mixed up with live ammunition on every corner and uniforms splattered with blood amongst the rubble. The

BORN ON THE WRONG SIDE OF THE FENCE

most horrible thing I saw was human bones minus flesh sticking out of half caved in cellar windows. They just could not make it as the fireball in the streets were thousands of degrees. With only superheated air around people who made it out of burning and collapsed buildings had no chance to survive. They melted instantly.

In nearly every street Austrian men and women under military supervision worked from morning to late afternoon cleaning the rubble from the roads. They cleaned the bricks of mortar by hand using a small ax, then stacked them by the thousands near the roads to be reused later for the rebuilding of Vienna. Steel beams, bent and molten glass were taken away for recycling. Not anything was thrown away. Brass fittings from taps and other items were reused again in later months. Those were the first few months after the war.

The feeding of those hard-working Austrians was the job of the occupying military forces. They brought the soup kitchen right up to the rubble heaps. Also they paid the weekly wages for each of the workers. So most of the streets of Vienna were cleared of rubble in the first two years.

Now Dad and Mum tracked through this rubble towards my Grandparents' home which luckily was only one kilometer from the Westbahnhof railway station. Dad left part of our luggage at the station for later collection. We could hardly believe our luck as we approached the street where my Grandparents lived. On one side of the street the houses were standing with only minor damage, but the other side was totally gone, bombed and collapsed, just meter high rubble for hundreds of meters.

God was with us. Grandpa's home was there looking fine and undamaged. Dad had tears running down his face and Mum was again nearly collapsing. We finally dragged her around the last corner into the Markt Graf Ruediger Strasse (Baron von Ruediger Street) Number One. Again the cold weather was having a very bad effect on Mum, and also we had no decent winter clothing. We climbed up to the second level in this wonderful old building which was built about 1835 in the Rococo style. Everything inside was handcrafted in finely hammered railings and beautiful rose marble slate stairs. Then the final moment had arrived. We knocked on the door. Grandma opened the beautiful carved door with inlaid leadlight glass panels and bronze handles. She just stood there in the dimly lit passage and not a word was said. Mum now collapsed into her arms, and Dad and Grandma dragged her into the bedroom. Finally after five minutes she and Grandpa came out and I never had so many hugs and kisses in my life. This also was repeated onto my little brother.

BORN ON THE WRONG SIDE OF THE FENCE

We were ushered into the apartment by Grandma, who was a small-built, big-busted lady of about 73 years of age. Her silver hair was combed straight back and tied into a large knot. I had not seen Grandma very much in my then young life, as I had spent most time with Grandma's daughter, Aunt Rosa, my father's sister, in Purkersdorf.

Grandpa Ehlich was the mayor before the war of a small city called Ebreichsdorf south of Vienna. As Grandpa Ehlich was a Nazi Party member, he lost his job as mayor in the last month of liberation by the Russian Army in 1945. I had absolutely forgotten his looks, but further, I had no recollection of the man himself. So it was for me a new beginning with my own grandparents.

It was very strange that Grandpa sent Grandma out to greet us while he stayed in his room. He finally approached after some five minutes and unceremoniously and unemotionally, without hugs or smiles, led us to the dining room/lounge. Oh, he was very happy to see Mum and Dad and my little brother Fritz. He was setting him on his lap, stroking Fritz's blond hair. It was then that I noticed that Grandpa had absolutely no love for me. I was glad that at least he had feelings for my brother, as Fritz was not well with his asthma. Grandma, however, was different. She really loved me and hugged me often.

We had to find out on the day of our arrival where we were to stay. Aunt Rosa's house in Purkersdorf was already chock full of our relatives. To make matters worse, the Russian occupation forces had made Aunt Rosa look after a Russian officer. More about that later. Aunt Anna also had an officer at that time in her little home. So what now? Here we were without a home. Grandpa wasn't very happy at all. He was not used to pressure of any kind. Vienna was bombed out completely and as hundreds and thousands of refugees returned, they were unable to find any living space. The rush was on to find a foothold anywhere for the time being. People were living in bombed out ruins, in cellars, anywhere there was shelter as wintertime was coming fast. Bombed out buildings were robbed for their destroyed doors and window frames and left over floorboards if they had survived the flames at all for firewood.

Grandma made Dad shift their brass double bed into the living/dining room including a huge wardrobe and one small one and her huge dressing table. We moved into their now empty bedroom. So now what? No beds? Dad stormed out of the apartment and one hour later dragged a double bed frame he had dug out from a burned out building into the apartment. The rusty old twisted bed was used for them. For the first night there was no mattress. We

BORN ON THE WRONG SIDE OF THE FENCE

boys slept on and in an ottoman settee which had a pull out drawer in the bottom. That was our bed for the next two years.

Chapter 14

Into the Cellar

Life was hard and we lived like thousands in this mad world on handouts, ration cards and luck. Dad started looking for a job and it did not take long for him as a mechanical engineer to obtain one. I do not know where or what he did until two years later. Every apartment owner or renter had a cellar partition and this was used mostly to store coal and firewood for the winter. Every room in those old buildings had a fireplace.

It was a long way down into the cellar and at least Grandpa with his aging body now had help. We boys had to collect timber again from bombed out buildings, bring it home, saw it and split and stack it. Then we had to run down into the cellar three flights down to fetch it up when they needed it.

At that time I was told that I had to start school again. I had missed by now exactly one full year of schooling due to the closure of the school in Leuchtenburg, Bavaria, and my service as a runner and helper for the German army. Mum took me days later to the school about one and a half kilometers from our apartment. Well, hardly had I started settling in, when I was in trouble. My German dialect did not go over well with the children and they said to me, "Go home, you Nazi Schwein!" Go home you Nazi pig. And before in Bavaria, Germany, they said, "Go home you Ostmark Schwein." Go home you Eastern pig. Now, at nearly ten years of age, this was a big blow for me. I went home crying and very upset. Dad took a day off work and he went to school with me. What he said to the headmaster I do not know, but knowing my father and the screaming coming out of the headmaster's office was an indication that things would be better from now on. Dad rushed out of the headmaster's office and into my classroom. There he cursed and yelled his head off to all the children. I must say no one could do this today as he would be arrested right away. But in those days it was dog eat dog, open warfare. The situation was resolved and I had no more trouble from then on.

One week later the first of many incidents started which nearly cost the life of my dear Grandma and Grandpa. First, I must tell you here, that when the bombing leveled the houses opposite our block of apartments it shattered all the windows in our home and Grandma's dining/living room. In our bedroom, the window was cracked in four places and the winter storms and winds whistled through the crack. Therefore Grandma decided to use paper sticky tape to cover the cracks. About 200 yards across from Grandma's window the Russian Army had about 500 men stationed. It was part of the postwar occupation force. They were looking right across the bombed out city block into our window. As Grandma applied the sticky tape onto the cracked glass, it must have appeared to the soldiers that we may have made a Swastika in German. Seconds later BANG! BANG! The glass in the window blasted into our room and covered Grandma with hundreds of glass splinters and a very nasty bullet graze on her right arm. The bullet, a nine millimeter slug, traveled across the room and lodged in Grandma's linen cupboard. I was in school and Dad was at work but Mum nearly had a miscarriage that day and Grandma had to call not only the police but also the doctor for her bullet wound. God was surely on her side. Grandpa was lucky as he was sleeping in our room on the sofa and did not even wake up! Well, this incident made the neighborhood rounds and the next day some angel turned up with some glass, putty and a cutting knife and the whole incident was forgotten, but written into the Ehlich family history book.

We struggled through wintertime and soon it was spring 1946. This year was and always will be the most memorable in my life as it brought with it trouble after trouble. Granddad was from early 1920 a member of the SA. As a Nazi Party member, the occupation he was practicing was that of an advocate, but most of his life he was to be the mayor of the city of Ebreichsdorf near Vienna.

So we struggled through very hard times, living together in the confinement of a very small apartment which comprised a very small kitchen, an entrance room, one toilet, one living room/lounge and one bedroom. As I had mentioned, we turned this living room/lounge into Grandpa and Grandma's bedroom and their bedroom into ours. So Dad, my pregnant Mum, my brother and I were confined into one space. There was no bathroom or showers in those 1835-built houses. Bathing was a weekly affair and was done in turns in the tiled kitchen using what was known in those days as a "sit-bath." It was a very small galvanized bathtub of about four feet long and one and a half feet wide with a higher backside. Usually Mum made the hot water in a large pot and this was transferred into the tub and then cold water was added. We children came first and starting with me (by now I was ten years old), I had to stand in the tub and Mum scrubbed me down. Any complaining

BORN ON THE WRONG SIDE OF THE FENCE

at all brought in my Dad and for a sure slap with his belt. Fritz, my little brother, was next, then Mum and Dad. The water by then had to be topped with hot water again. Next Dad emptied the bathtub and refilled it again with fresh water for Grandma and Grandpa. This happened every weekend.

Now to our weekly and daily washing routines. We did our washing in an enameled hand basin. Mum and Grandma did their weekly laundry in the bathtub with a scrubbing board. The washing and rinsing was hard enough, but the drying was a massive job. Dad had rigged up small hooks between the window frames and Mum strung some small ropes from one hook to the one opposite and then the washing was hung using the open windows. In wintertime the windows were shut and the drying took much longer. By late springtime it was easier.

I was the only1 one to attend church not far from our home. I was proud that I was allowed to be an altar boy. Nobody from my family ever went to church. They had lost faith in God seeing all that slaughter during the war.

In the early summer Mum took us to the local bathhouse where we had our weekly scrub-up. There I had my first experience of seeing a gentleman committing suicide by slashing his wrists in his bathtub. I happened to see this as the bath master opened this bathroom. The time had run out for this man to use this bathroom and we were next in line. When he opened the bath room, I saw this blue body floating in this blood red water and the tiles in the bathroom were splattered from top to bottom with blood as he must have thrashed around in his death throes. My pregnant Mum had to sit down and recover for quite a long time. But in later weeks she never booked that particular bath room again. I have never forgotten this bloody incident; as shortly afterwards this dramatic incident was to be repeated in our own home.

By now summertime had arrived in Vienna and Mum was in her last month of pregnancy. She could not do what she usually did. I had to do a lot of work after school, on top of my homework. Like shopping at the corner shop. There were no supermarkets in those days. Also fetching firewood from the cellar, cutting and chopping wood down in the cellar. Do this and do that. Any back talk to Mum and Dad would strap me when he came home very tired late in the evening. He himself was very tired out as he had to walk to work every day. No trams, no buses, no trains, nothing. All was smashed up and all had to be rebuilt in those postwar days. So one day on a rainy weekend Dad told us boys to go down into the cellar to cut up some firewood into manageable lengths. As the cellar deep below the building had no electric lights, we had to use candles. And believe me, the cellar was really deep below street level. It was about sixty steps winding down in a very small stairwell. The damp and musty smell one can never forget. We boys were really frightened down there as we had heard stories that robbers and murderers used these underground passages for hideouts.

These cellars and passages traveled underground from one building to the next. During the war the walls were cut through so in case one building was bombed the people who used the cellars as air raid shelters could escape into the next building. As I explained earlier, people who used those cellars were drowned and gassed to death. The passages filled with water from broken water mains, broken gas mains and smoke from the burning houses.

Into these frightening surroundings we went. No wonder we boys nearly fainted with fright. Then there were those shadows of our bodies reflected onto the wet tunnel wall. I laugh today remembering the way we used to work, me and my little brother. Me cutting the timbers and splitting them and my brother standing watch and looking into the dark passage. He was really afraid of ghosts, moreso than I. So when we were ready to carry up a load of firewood he walked up in front of me and I walked backwards with the flickering candle. Up the sixty stairs we went with one hand holding the firewood and in the other the candle. Finally we arrived on the first floor totally breathless and shaking so we took a rest by placing the firewood on the landing. While we rested there and recovered, my father came down from the second floor, screaming and cursing us because we took so long.

We explained to him that we were afraid down there in the cellar. What did our war hero Dad do? He slapped us in our face and kicked us in the bottom for admitting to being frightened. Suddenly the first floor resident, a school professor, opened his door and asked my father why we boys were being treated this way. He had no right to slap us around for only admitting to being frightened down there in the cellar. It was obvious that he had heard all this through his closed door. What did my father do? He dropped this professor with a swift punch to the chin so fast that I didn't even see his hand move. Only in later years did I find out that Dad was an amateur boxer in his college days.

Through all this commotion someone had called the police just around the corner from us. Dad was arrested and spent four days in jail. He had to publicly apologize to this poor professor and he was lucky that he was not jailed longer. That was the first time that I had seen the other side of my father's temper. I was told he acquired this during his war experiences from all the slaughter he had seen. I want to only mention this here as in later years we will see his temper led to his mental illness.

Life was very hard. Living space was hard to get as most buildings were bombed out in Vienna. So residents living in an undamaged house with spare rooms had by law people without a home living with them and they were called "Untermieter." Worst of all no rent had to be paid to the landlord. These were the conditions months after the war. So short were accommodations that people slept and lived in bombed out homes. The owners were either dead or had left. People lived in cellars or deep below Vienna in the catacombs. Especially in the cold Nordic winters with no electricity, gas or coal. It was terror. People just used up every scrap of timber they could find or dig out of the bombed ruins.

During those hard times suicides were plentiful and families who survived the whole war committed this frightening act not only to themselves, no, they killed their children too.

One lovely day as I was coming home from school and looking forward to playing with my little brother, I was confronted with a terrible scene. The front door of our apartment was open and outside stood about five or more residents of the upper and lower floors. They had Mum and Grandma between them and were hugging them and stroking their heads.

I asked, "What's the matter, and why are Mum and Grandma crying?" I was told that Grandpa was in the hospital and may be dying as he attempted to kill himself in our toilet by slashing his wrist. My father, who had come home early, saw the blood pouring out underneath the toilet door. He smashed open the door and found Grandpa slumped over the toilet half dead. He tourniqueted Grandpa's hands and carried him downstairs to the police station where the French medics were called. They rushed Grandpa to a military hospital.

Later that day after Mum had settled down I was told the very bad news that caused my grandfather to do what he did. Early in the afternoon there was a knock on the door and after opening the door Grandma and Mum were confronted by several French military personnel and amongst them a French and German interpreter. They asked if Grandpa was home as they wanted to speak to him urgently.

Sensing trouble, Grandpa invited them to his sitting/bedroom where he offered them a drink. To his astonishment they denied this invitation and came straight to the point. The person in charge was a female French Army officer, very arrogant, and through the interpreter she told Grandpa that due to his

BORN ON THE WRONG SIDE OF THE FENCE

involvement in the Nazi Party and in the Brownshirts (the SA) his apartment was to be confiscated by the French military and that he and his family had 24 hours to vacate the premises. Grandma had to catch Grandpa as he nearly passed out. Sitting down on a chair, he had to sign a document releasing the apartment to the French military. I must state here that Grandpa had always lived in sponsored living quarters, as he'd always been involved in politics and the Nazi Party. Also, 25 years' service as mayor of Ebreichsdorf entitled him to a very nice large house. However, Grandpa and Grandma had a share in my aunt's villa in Purkersdorf in the Vienna woods. Unfortunately this villa was now partly occupied by several Russian officers and my aunt's own extended family. Grandpa therefore chose to end his life rather than to ask Aunt Rosa and Uncle Hans for help. The loss of the war, the loss of his job, his friends, his luxurious lifestyle and now his apartment drove him over the edge. We all prayed that he would survive. It would take nearly four weeks in that military hospital and then several weeks treatment in Vienna's Steinhof Mental Hospital for him to be released back home.

In the meantime my Dad and Aunt Rosa's husband had to find a horse and cart to transfer Grandma and Grandpa's furniture and meager belongings to Purkersdorf, a thirty-kilometer trip. The poor horse could have been two horses. I never found out. So at least Grandma and Grandpa were squeezed into the villa. Thanks to God for Grandpa's old mates. They found him a new council flat months later. Due to Mum's advanced pregnancy, the French military found us a small room not far away and as we had only a hand cart of belongings, the transfer was an easy one.

Our new home was about a half a kilometer from our now lost apartment and situated in a very large and wide street called Neubaugurtlel. Ninety percent of all houses here were bombed and burned out buildings in collapsible states. The underground tram system was not working and somehow the street tram cars were actually coming on line by now. The streets were still covered with rubble meters high. I had by now half a kilometer more to go to school, which I really did not like. So one way to school took me half an hour, but walking uphill.

Back to our new living quarters. Our one room measured nine feet wide and fifteen feet long, with one window looking into an internal yard. On the second floor level in that building the people who had to supply this room to the French military were business people by the name of Obratowisch and they had a hairdressing salon not far away and across the road. Mrs. Obratowisch was at that time about 50 and a widow who had lost her husband

BORN ON THE WRONG SIDE OF THE FENCE

in the war. She had a twenty year old daughter named Milli. Milli really liked me. She loved music and her hobby was listening to records on this old wind-up gramophone. And as any young person today, she had a favorite LP called "Kleine Frau Warum So Traurig" (Little Woman, Why Are You So Sad?"), which she played day in and day out. Today after 60 years I still remember those words.

Our room was cold and musty and to our dismay there was no stove to heat up the room. Our furniture was a double bed and one ottoman lounge with a pull out drawer in which my brother slept, as I slept on the lounge above. In the mornings my brother came out of the drawer and the bedding went inside. Also there was one small wooden table and four chairs Dad had made out of boxes, and a wardrobe, that's it. We had to fetch the water from outside as the apartment had no bathroom.

Again Mum dragged us to the bath house. In this terrible situation, the worst I ever had, my sister was born. I remember the first day Mum brought Evie home. Dad warmed up the milk which he received from the Red Cross on a candle stuck in an old jam tin. It took nearly half an hour to warm this ice cold milk. That was the first time I overheard Mum saying to Dad it would be better if they would turn the gas on in Mrs. Obratowisch's kitchen and put us all out of misery. I never found out if she actually meant to do it or she just joked. But I really was terrified as what I had seen with my grandfather was enough for me. Luckily my father had a job and in the next few weeks things improved. We even had a primitive electric heater for warming and cooking.

Next to our city block was a public park called Marz Park (March Park). God only knows how this park received its name. Right in the middle of it was a huge underground concrete bunker that rose about eight meters above street level. This bunker had all its entrances sealed up with earth and rocks and grass was growing all over. Since the end of the war children used this bunker (it was now one year since the war had ended) to play hide and seek or to go skating down its steep sides. I used to drag up my little baby sister in her pram and my brother was standing below. As the pram with my sister in it rolled down the steep sides, I would give the pram a little push to send it downhill by itself with my baby sister in it. Evie used to like this as she screamed with delight. Could it have been terror for her? Then one day as I passed the park after school I noticed that they were constructing a six foot high timber fence around the park which of course included our play bunker. Sadly I watched every day as slowly the day approached which spelled the end of our playground. The park was fully enclosed.

BORN ON THE WRONG SIDE OF THE FENCE

One full week passed. Then I heard a muffled explosion inside the fence. Well, I thought, they must have blasted open the entrances of the bunker. I wasn't far off. The whole roof of the bunker was blasted away. Actually they used only enough explosives to crack the roof shell. Then, using heavy machinery, the digging began.

I never expected what I would discover in the next few days. Later I passed again and tried to find a crack in the fence to see what was going on inside. As I did so I stumbled upon one of the most horrifying scenes in my then young life. I had seen such scenes before in the concentration camps in Germany days after the war ended and in Magdeburg during the bombing. What I stumbled upon here was both shocking and unexpected. Just in front of my feet, protruding out and underneath the fence, was a human hand, partly decomposed with shreds of skin hanging off the fingers which were all partly covered in a totally blood-soaked Russian uniform. The hand was connected to a decomposed body. It was too large to pass underneath the fence. I stood there frozen and tried hard not to scream. Then I saw just in front of the pointing ring finger a gleaming gold wedding ring protruding out of the clay and sandy ground. I realized that they must have opened a mass grave full of decomposing bodies and as they excavated them by machinery, one was flung forward and partly under the fence.

As I recovered my spinning senses I picked up that ring and ran as fast as I could around the corner. Guess who I ran into. My Dad coming home from work. "Dad! Dad!" I said. "Come and I'll show you something," and then I produced that gold ring.

"Where did you get that from?" he asked, and pulled the ring right out of my hand.

"Dad, come with me," I said. "There is a dead body part sticking out underneath the park fence."

"Okay," he said, and we walked around the corner towards the decomposing hand. To my surprise he laughed and kicked the hand back underneath the fence. "It's just what I need," he said, and stuck the ring in his pocket. Later I found out that Dad melted that ring and had a gold crown made for his front tooth. He later told me that it was a war injury, and God made it up to him, of course, with a big smile.

Weeks later I was told that that bunker contained nearly one thousand bodies of German, Austrian and Russian soldiers who died in the fierce fighting around Vienna; also bodies of civilian bombing victims. The available three-story deep bunker was very handy for a quick temporary grave.

BORN ON THE WRONG SIDE OF THE FENCE

    Two months passed by. Then they removed the fence and behold, there was no sign of any bunker having been there at all. Just nice green grass and a playground for the children. That's life. "Here today, gone tomorrow." However, I was told that all the dead had been transferred to their respective cemeteries and buried with full honors. Bodies with identifications were sent back to Russia or their relatives in Austria, Germany and other places. Then a year later a memorial was erected in that park honoring the fallen soldiers and civilians in that awful last battle for Vienna.

BORN ON THE WRONG SIDE OF THE FENCE

Chapter 15

The Missing Children

Slowly Vienna took on a more civilized appearance. Trams started to run, and the underground was running partly to some of Vienna's 21 suburbs. Buses and taxis started to appear again. Still, the rubble of burned-out buildings was everywhere. I just struggled through school. By losing one full year of schooling in Germany in the last year of the war, it took a toll on me. I just could not catch up.

We had a butcher shop in our building and the owner was a very respectable, friendly person. Mum sometimes asked him if she could pay for the daily meat when Dad got paid. He always obliged Mum and in return Mum fixed his uniform when it was torn. His butcher shop was neat and clean and it came as a surprise when one morning the shop was closed.

There was a sign saying "until further notice." However, the shop never reopened. Mum and all the other customers had to walk a kilometer to the next butcher. What had happened to the nice butcher? We thought his business was good and he had lots of customers. With the supply of meat so short after the war, that might have had some effect on his closing, but did it? Surprise! Surprise! We did not have to wait too long to find out what happened. One day the police asked questions of his ex-customers, wanting to know if they had noticed anything funny about the meat he had sold lately. Yes, some said, the meat tasted a bit sweet and had a different feel and color. Weeks later, we read in the newspaper that the butcher was to be hanged for killing his wife and disposing of her by selling her meat to his unsuspecting customers. He would have gotten away with it for sure if it were not his bad luck that one of his customers was a lady pathologist. One day after purchasing several pounds of meat at his butcher shop, she noticed by the shape and color that this meat was human. She took it to the laboratory at work and confirmed her suspicion. She notified the police immediately, and they broke into his freezer only to discover the upside down body of his wife hanging on a hook amongst other animal meats. The body had already been partly sold to customers. After the war in Austria, the death sentence was still

BORN ON THE WRONG SIDE OF THE FENCE

used for murders and established war crimes and rapes. Therefore our good butcher was hanged, but not in his freezer.

Unforgettable is this unbelievable horror story, which unfolded in early 1947 in the last month before we made our next major residential move and thanks to God away from the rubble and misery of burned out Vienna. As I mentioned before, I had to walk to school quite a long way. This, however, was very pleasant during the summer or springtime, but not so in autumn or winter.

It all started one day in school. All the pupils and teachers were called into the school's gymnasium. There we were surprised to see amongst our teachers several high ranking policemen and policewomen. They assembled on the stage and seated themselves. Our headmaster introduced all the police personnel and outlined roughly the reason for the urgency of this meeting. The senior policeman and policewoman took center stage and with very serious and stern-looking faces they explained that in the last few months, several children attending this school were missing. By "missing" they explained that the children had never returned home after school.

Nobody, including the police, had any idea what had happened to those children. Most of them were under the age of 12. We, the students, were asked for input or if we saw or knew anything at all. After about half an hour the meeting was ended due to lack of evidence or knowledge of anything regarding this matter.

Later in the week, two more students went missing from a school nearby. The disappearances only stopped momentarily as parents walked their children to school and picked them up after school. However, on weekends more children went missing. All in all, 20 children had disappeared in our district alone. Parents started to keep their children at home now and wherever their children had to go, their mother or father followed. School attendance was down as children stayed home. Vienna's newspapers were full of ideas. The police and detectives worked around the clock. Then one lovely sunny hot summer day, Vienna awoke to church bells ringing and newspapers with blaring headlines, "CHILDREN FOUND DEAD!" Vienna came to an abrupt halt. People could not get enough information. The newspapers were all sold in minutes. Churches were full to the brim with people praying for those dead children.

What had happened? The story unfolded like this. Several weeks earlier one very young-looking lady detective, with the backup of several other detectives, tried something not attempted before. She had her blond hair

BORN ON THE WRONG SIDE OF THE FENCE

arranged in plaits like a nine- to thirteen-year-old Austrian schoolgirl and wore a typical Austrian schoolgirl's dress: white blouse, blue skirt, white knee socks and high-laced shoes. With a leather schoolbag on her back, she tramped the streets in our suburb up and down for days. She was followed by three armed male detectives. One morning as she pretended to be on her way to school, she walked past an open doorway of a four-story high partly burned out office building. Standing next to the doorway was a blind person. I must say here that in Germany and Austria, blind people wear a yellow armband around their right arm. If a person is totally blind, this armband has three large black dots printed in a triangle on it. This all children learn in school and they are taught to be very helpful and kind to those persons.

Respectfully, our lady detective said "Gruss Gott," meaning greetings from God, an everyday common German or Austrian greeting. The blind person, an elderly male, respectfully replied with the same greetings, but added, "Please, little girl, would you be so kind as to deliver an envelope upstairs to the third floor, to Number 14. Please, as you can see I am unable to do this myself. Just knock on the door upstairs and a lady will open. Just give it to her, my darling little child."

Our lady detective here had the suspicion that somehow something was very unusual about his request. However, she obliged his demand, but being very careful decided to arm her small revolver under her skirt. She also knew that her partners must have seen her entering the building. Later they told the story that they had seen her talking to a blind man, but as she entered the building he took off his armband and ran away so fast that it was obvious to them something was very wrong. So hastily they followed her upstairs.

When she reached No. 14, our lady detective knocked on the door and she observed that she also was being observed through a spy hole in the door. The door was opened by an apparently old-looking lady who asked her to put the letter just inside on a small table. As she did that, the door slammed shut behind her and two men stormed out of one room. As they took hold of her, she put her hand under her skirt and pulled the trigger. One of the men collapsed on the floor, having been shot in the stomach. As the second shot was fired, the other man fled through the front door only to be confronted by our good detectives who were just about to smash the door in. He was shot straight through his leg and also collapsed. Our old looking lady turned out to be a third male accomplice. He was apprehended without a struggle.

What confronted the three detectives now was the biggest, and I mean biggest, horror story ever told at that time. By entering the rooms in that apartment, they discovered human carved-up body parts hanging on butcher hooks. In another room there was a complete running soap factory in full swing and complete machinery set up for making canned dog and cat food. To top this, the blood-spattered bathroom was waiting for her, our lady detective. Going into too many details here would sicken one's stomach. To cut this story short, after recuperating and a short trial, all three were hanged in Vienna's jail. There was a huge funeral for all of the slaughtered children. People never knew if they had washed themselves with this soap or fed their animals with that pet food. Much of that was confiscated after the arrests. All three male criminals later were discovered to have been SS guards from that dreaded concentration camp Treblinka in Poland. We children went back to school and were told the whole story, and believe me it was the best lesson in my young life: Not to trust anybody.

Austria and Germany were bad places after the war because so many war criminals and murderers were running freely about. For me, I just say what I saw in the concentration camp in Flossenburg makes my stomach turn when someone says to me, "OH, THAT NEVER HAPPENED." So as I sat in a 707 one day many years later and one reporter showed me the pictures of handcuffed Iranian child combatants lying on the ground in one line and an Iraqi tank driving over their young heads. WHAT, THAT NEVER HAPPENED! What a joke! What, four thousand Polish officers cut down by machine gun fire by the Russians during the Stalin period? WHAT, THAT NEVER HAPPENED! God please look after them. Many people I have met in my life who said to me, "Bruno, it can't be that you experienced all this." I wish God had spared me all this. Believe me my friends, this is nothing compared to what the brave U.S. and Allied soldiers, Marines, sailors and airmen went through by giving their lives and souls and health to deliver us Germans and Austrians and many more nations from the dreaded Nazis. For me personally, I thank the 90th Division for their deeds, as you have seen in previous pages.

GOD BLESS THEM ALL

P.S. This ends the period between 1936 and 1947. Thereafter I had no more contact with the GIs of the mighty U.S. Army, as my family settled down in the Russian occupation sector.

I personally thank Glenn and Vern Schmidt for their help, research and giving me the encouragement to continue writing. I myself and my wife Josie developed a beautiful relationship with these beautiful men and their beloved wives. Of course I will continue writing my memories for a long time yet.

BORN ON THE WRONG SIDE OF THE FENCE

However, I just would like these first few chapters to be published in the U.S. to thank especially the 90th Division. However, as we could not establish the whereabouts of those tankers in Leuchtenburg, Bavaria, near Weiden, I consider these chapters still unfinished, until further research. Then a further amendment would be published.
GOD BLESS AMERICA

Bruno Ehlich, Sgt. (retired) RAAF, Australia

BORN ON THE WRONG SIDE OF THE FENCE

Postscript

From 761st.com:

"November 11, 2006 – Sixty-one years ago in a German village named Leuchtenburg, WWII was winding down at a fast pace. A nine year old Hitler Youth kid, named Bruno Ehlich, was an ammunition carrier on a German anti-tank gun positioned in the woods just outside this village. Their orders from the SS soldiers were to fire on any oncoming American tanks hoping to slow down their advance. An American Sherman tank rumbled up into view and Bruno's crew fired on this tank but caused no damage. Return fire from the tank wiped out the German crew, either killed or wounded. Bruno, wounded and scared, ran to the castle in this village only to find the SS troops gone, now leaving the defense of Leuchtenburg in the hands of those Hitler Youths.

"Bruno, running from the castle down to the village center, found himself staring up into the huge barrel of the 76 gun on the tank. A black tanker jumped to the ground, grabbed Bruno by the neck, and demanded to know the location of the German troops or where they were hiding. Bruno revealed a secret underground passage and shortly the village was in American hands and little nine year old Bruno found himself a prisoner of this black tanker.

"Bruno's story, "Born on the Wrong Side of the Fence," written in 2004, had a chapter missing. Who was this black GI tanker? Was he still alive? Can I find him or his unit? Persistent searching by Vern Schmidt, a combat veteran of the 0-th Infantry Division and a friend of Bruno, found Joe Wilson, Jr., author of the book "The 761st 'Black Panther' Tank Battalion in World War II." Joe's father was in this unit and was familiar with much of its history through France and German, and Joe Wilson Jr. became very involved in trying to find the tanker who had grabbed Bruno on that April day back in 1945.

"Following several phone calls to Mr. Johnnie Stevens, Jr., of Carteret, N.J., and he being a former tanker from the 761st Tank Battalion, Mr. Stevens said, "I believe that probably was me." Now, after sixty one years, Bruno Ehlich, a retired Sergeant from the Royal Australian Air Force, sent Mr.

BORN ON THE WRONG SIDE OF THE FENCE

Johnnie Stevens, Jr. a letter of congratulation and thanked him for liberating this little Austrian kid from Hitler's Nazi army.

"Poor health and continents apart will probably prevent these two gentlemen from meeting each other, but perhaps now Bruno can realize his long search is complete. Our congratulations to Mr. Johnnie Stevens, Jr. on receiving the coveted French National Legion of Honor award for his exemplary service in WWII to the French people. May God Bless Johnnie Stevens, Jr., Vern Schmidt, 90th Infantry Division, World War II."

Johnnie Stevens, Jr. *Credit: 761st.com*

Post Postscript

October 2015 – 90th Infantry Division member Vernon Schmidt reports tht although he questioned whether 761st tankers came into Leuchtenburg on the 24th of April of 1945, because that was in the 90th Infantry Division area and the 90th set up a divisional command post at 4:00 p.m. on the 24th in that little town in Bavaria, several veterans told him that African American tankers were there. He was recently told by a WWII vet that the 71st Infantry Division was just west of Leuchtenburg that day, and he confirmed that the 761st was supporting them. Vernon's thinking is that a 761st tank may have gone down a road that led into the 90th area. As a funny side note, one of the men asked a Hitler Youth (Vernon's post-war friend, Bruno Ehlich) where the German soldiers were. Bruno showed them a hidden passage into the castle, and when the tank guys blew the lock off the door to this passage all kinds of people came out, including a lady whose sons were on an anti-tank gun trying to stop the tank. She had a pistol in her hand and pointed it at the tank like she was going to take it prisoner, since she was made at the Americans for what they did to her sons on the anti-tank gun. Vernon has been back there four times, staying in a guest house that was then owned by the same lady.

An added note: After Action Reports show "A Company, 357th Regiment, 90th Infantry Division, entering Leuchtenburg on 24 April 1945 and setting up a Divisional Command Post. No doubt Johnnie Stevens and his "Black Panthers" moved on to take the next village.

Bruno Ehlich died on June 7, 2013. He was 77 years old. Johnnie Stevens died on July 12, 2007. He was 86 years old. Although Bruno did finally learn who his liberator was, he and Johnnie Stevens, Jr. never met after the war.

BORN ON THE WRONG SIDE OF THE FENCE

Also from Chi Chi Press:

UP ABOVE THE CLOUDS TO DIE

A tragic error. An epic battle. An oral history
The Kassel Mission of 27 Sept. 1944

By AARON ELSON

BORN ON THE WRONG SIDE OF THE FENCE

EXPANDED THIRD EDITION

TANKS

for the memories

The 712th Tank Battalion during World War II

by Aaron Elson

Visit https://aaronelson.com

FROM PARATROOPER TO PUBLIC DEFENDER

Reflections of a 103-year-old World War II veteran

By MORTON KATZ

With Aaron Elson

BORN ON THE WRONG SIDE OF THE FENCE

PRISONERS OF WAR
An Oral History

By Aaron Elson

BORN ON THE WRONG SIDE OF THE FENCE

Podcast:
War As My Father's Tank Battalion Knew It. Host: Aaron Elson
https://myfatherstankbattalion.com

Made in the USA
Middletown, DE
22 September 2024